Chapman 81

Elspeth Davie and the (

Cover photograph: Michael Knowles

Illustrations:
Tash MacLeod, Alasdair Gray

ISBN 0 906772 67 2   ISSN 0308-2695   © Chapman 1995

CHAPMAN
4 Broughton Place, Edinburgh EH1 3RX, Scotland
Tel 0131–557 2207   Fax 0131–556 9565
Editor: Joy Hendry   Associate Editor: Robert Calder
Production: Peter Cudmore   Advertising & Marketing: Mary Gordon
Volunteers: Majella Hackett, Eva Hartmann, Julie McCulloch

Submissions:
Chapman welcomes submissions of poetry,
fiction and articles provided they are
accompanied by a stamped addressed envelope
or International Reply Coupons

Subscriptions:

	Personal		Institutional	
	1 year	2 years	1 year	2 years
UK	£13	£25	£17	£30
Overseas	£17/$30	£30/$57	£21/$37	£39/$68

SAC logo: Centre between text
above and below; justify against left
edge of text directly above

Edinburgh DC logo: Centre between
text above and below; justify against
right edge of table directly above

Printed by Mayfair Printers, Print House, Commercial Road, Sunderland, Tyne & Wear

Notes on the Short Story

Elspeth Davie

One of the difficulties, I think, for anyone talking about the way he writes or any other person writes is that in the doing of this thing there is a mixture of the highly conscious and the totally unconscious. That's to say, there is one part he can talk about and explain – the other he can't. One might go on about technique, literary forms, creative consciousness, metaphor, etc., but where the actual imagination comes from and what it *is* is rather a mystery. Many people have tried to describe it. Coleridge, in a characteristically impassioned passage, speaks of Shakespeare's imagination as "the creative power and the intellectual energy wrestling as in a war embrace." But as we are going to be discussing writing today – the short story in particular – may I, as one theme, put forward the suggestion that it is the *limitations* – sometimes quite painful ones – imposed on a writer (indeed on any artist) that give him his special kind of freedom and that can sometimes release his imagination like the releasing of a tightly-held-down spring. Indeed he may try to ignore these limitations at his peril.

Taking the story, although it is short or perhaps *because* it is short, there is room in it for many things. It can have great gulfs of space inside it. There is room in it for strange contrasts and oppositions. It can have great depth, or perhaps the word should be intensity. Often it can contain silence and always it has those sudden flashes or shocks of recognition and awareness. In really great writers this imagination, this awareness is so powerful it comes off the page like an electric shock. Eugene Ionesco has said: "To tear ourselves away from everyday habit, from mental laziness which hides us from the strangeness of reality, we must receive something like a bludgeon blow." These shocks or bludgeon blows in good writing are of course nothing to do with sensationalism. Sometimes, indeed, they are very quiet things – subdued bits of writing expressing intense silence, space or deep emotion. Sometimes our characters are not able to use words at all. I am reminded of a passage in Henry James' *Portrait of a Lady* where a man and a woman are talking together. The man says something to the woman. She doesn't answer, says nothing at all, but simply puts up her fan to hide the expression on her face. This moves us because it is something we recognise – our fear of the inadequacy of words plus the need to disguise the sharpness of an emotion.

Or the sudden shocks of awareness can appear in the comic or tragic juxtaposition of something routine or sober set against a mad and turbulent background. Let us think for a moment of Joseph Conrad's 'Typhoon' – a long story certainly but with the usual limitations of its kind. We have the picture of Captain McWhirr – a very solid, responsible and undemonstrative man sitting in his chartroom on board ship writing one of his innumerable letters home to his wife who couldn't care less what ocean he's on and only hopes he won't be back too soon and ruin her tea parties. He is writing his letter just before the start of a terrific typhoon, "My darling wife," he begins, as all his letters begin, "the weather has been very fine this trip." Now the storm crashes upon the ship and we have this odd, domestic image of the captain:

> Very grave, straddling his legs far apart, and stretching his neck, he started to tie deliberately the strings of his sou'wester under his chin, with thick fingers that trembled slightly. He went through all the movements of a woman putting on her bonnet before a glass, with a strained, listening attention as though he had expected every moment to hear the shout of his name in the confused clamour that had suddenly beset his ship.

There are, of course, endless instances of the flashes and shocks which alert us and which are the essence of the short story – flashes silent as lightning. Amongst longer and more involved passages in Herman Melville's *Billy Budd* we are suddenly alerted by this straightforward and seemingly commonplace sentence appearing on the page: "What is the matter with the master-at-arms?" And we know by a sort of eerie frisson that there is something deep and mysterious about this man, later revealed to be his bitter envy of the good which he perceives in the young sailor, Billy Budd, who has joined the ship – an envy which also has in it the possibility of love. Melville describes Claggart, the master-at-arms, by saying that to pass from a normal nature to the nature of this man one must pass "the deadly space between". I have always felt that sentence beginning "What was the matter..." rather awful – in the real meaning of that word – perhaps because we use the phrase so often in everyday life.

Interestingly enough, it is occasionally those writers whose mother tongue is not British who have a special care for the words of our language, for example Nabokov who wrote all his early stories in Russian but became a master of style in English. Also Borges, the Argentinian, Karen Blixen or Isak Dineson, the Dane, who wrote most of her finest stories in English, and of course Joseph Conrad who was Polish, and Isaac Bashevis Singer who wrote his early stories in Yiddish. Perhaps the strains and discipline of mastering another language made them particularly conscious of style, gave them a special relish for words not familiar to them from birth.

For words, like shells, are not limited by their hard outline. They have intricate patterns evolved through aeons of time. They are objects encrusted with ancient stuff – plants, minerals and other shells: they have once contained a living creature, and so on. Words, too, bring echoes from distant shores of the world, from living languages and forgotten tongues. They may have meanings from various trades and professions. I was looking up the word "ingrained" the other day in the sense of being ineradicable. It is a word from the dying trade. The dried bodies of cochineal insects were used to produce a brilliant red dye. An example comes from Shakespeare's *Twelfth Night* when Olivia unveils her face to Viola and Viola who is disguised as a man, says: "Tis excellently done, if God did all." Olivia replies: "Tis in grain, sir, 'twill endure wind and weather."

We have thought about the space and silence that can be expressed in a short story, and I am thinking of James Joyce's 'The Dead' when at the end Gabriel is by a window at night, watching the snow falling gradually and silently over the great empty spaces of Ireland.

> It was falling on every part of the dark central plain, on the treeless hills, falling softly upon the Bog of Allen and, further westward, softly falling into the dark mutinous Shannon waves. It was falling too on every part of the lonely churchyard on the hill where Michael lay buried. It lay thickly drifted on the crooked crosses and headstones, on the spears of the little gate, on the barren thorns. His soul swooned slowly as he heard the snow falling faintly through the universe and faintly falling, like the descent of their last end, upon all the living and the dead.

But I must not be tempted to speak all the time about reading. Our title, I think, is the pleasures and pitfalls of *writing* short stories. Perhaps the first great pleasure comes when we suddenly feel we've a great idea for a story. We are excited. It burst on us "out of the blue", we say. We have to be careful of that blue. For like all pleasures we want to expand it, enlarge it at once. We wish to put everything we've got into the idea, everything we know and feel, see every side of it, and worst of all, perhaps, tell everyone about it. We would like to respond in a friendly way to the question: "What is your story going to be about?" Flannery O'Connor, whom we shall speak about again, said:

> People have a habit of saying: "What is the theme of your story?" And they expect you to give them a statement: "The theme of my story is the economic pressure of the machine on the middle class" or some such thing. And when they get a statement like that they go off happy and feel it is no longer necessary to read the story. Some people have the notion that you read the story and then climb out of it into its meaning, but for the writer the whole story is the meaning, because it is an experience, not an abstraction.

The trouble is that if we put too much pressure on our idea, looking at it from every angle, analysing what it means – the life may seem to run out of it. It may become unwieldy, shapeless. And whatever else the short story is it must try to have a very definite shape. Perhaps it's like making a sound piece of pottery. It must stand up, that's to say. It must have a right balance.

The strange and rather disturbing thing about all the creative arts, even those that look the most free and exuberant, is that a certain coolness and distance has gone into the making of them. I sometimes think writing a story is like looking into a lighted window in passing – you see an interesting scene inside, warm, moving and intense, but severely framed as far as you, the spectator outside, is concerned. That is to say you have to be a little distant from it to put it in focus. You are not of the company, so to speak. And yet the paradox in all the arts is that warmth and excitement of some kind must always be in you to enable you to write at all. So here we have to deal with an idea which we must be excited about without being totally carried away. The phrase "being carried away" reminds me that we must keep a cool and rather wary look at where we're going in the story. Particularly, of course, we must have a glimpse of the end of the journey even though it may be through a mist to begin with. Otherwise the original exciting idea isn't going to see us through. It might disappear after a few miles and then we'll really panic. A short story, to tell the truth, is seldom an easy amble along a well-marked lane. More often it's a bit of a tightrope walk, a balancing act over a sort of Niagara of sights, sounds and sensations that we'd love to look down at, but can't in case we fall off the wire. We have to get across, and what's more, do it with a certain amount of grace. I'm aware that almost everything one says about writing can have a sort of built-in contradiction because writers have such very different temperaments and aims. While I talk bout coolness and keeping a certain distance I have to remember Kafka's words to a young man who had shown him some short stories:

> Yours is a hesitant groping for the world. But in time that will cease and then perhaps your outstretched hand will withdraw as if caught by fire. Perhaps you will cry out, stammer incoherently or grind your teeth and open your eyes wide, very wide. At present these are only words. But art is a matter of the entire personality.

So to go back, the short story writer has to work within very different limits of time and space, and he feels all the cramping difficulties of communication under these circumstances. What he tries to do, what he must do if he is any kind of an artist, is to take out of the chaos around him only certain things that have moved him – sounds, images, the words and silences between persons – things which he instinctively relates in some way and rearranges so as to make a complete story. He, as it were, stands his ground. He cannot allow himself to be redirected or loaded up with things which are no part of the main story. Anton Tchekov was saying something about this when he wrote to a friend:

> You write that the hero of my story ['The Name Day Party'] is a figure worth developing. Good Lord, I am not an insentient brute. To tell you the truth I would have been only too glad to spend half a year on the story. I would gladly describe *all* my hero, describe him with feeling, understanding and deliberation. I'd describe his emotions when his wife was in labour. I'd describe the midwife and the doctors having tea in the middle of the night. I'd describe the rain... It would be sheer pleasure because I love digging deep and rummaging. But what can I do? I began the story on Sept 10 with the thought that I have to finish it by Oct 4th at the latest.

Of course Tchekov is talking on one level about deadlines, but he is also talking about selection, the importance to him of a certain ruthlessness in leaving out material, interesting enough in itself, but which he had not felt to be a necessary part of the whole thing he had in mind.

Tchekov wrote many letters about his work – mostly to editors, other writers and would-be writers. It seems strange nowadays to realise that he came under a good deal of criticism for his subject-matter. We remember that he was a good doctor and that some of the incidents and the detail in his stories came from the side of him that was the observant medical man. Here he is answering one such criticism:

But the writer is not a pastry-chef, he is not a cosmetician and not an entertainer. He is a man bound by contract to his sense of duty. He is just like an ordinary reporter. What would you say of a newspaper reporter who, as a result of squeamishness or a desire to please his readers, was to limit his descriptions to honest City Fathers, high-minded ladies and virtuous railwaymen: To the chemist there is nothing impure on earth. The writer should be as objective as the chemist. He should acknowledge that the manure piles play a highly respectable role in the landscape and that evil passions are every bit as much a part of life as good ones.

It isn't always remembered, when we've a pen in our hands and are staring at a piece of blank paper, that a writer must also be continually listening – in his inner ear – to whatever he's working on, long or short. He is listening to the rhythm. He is aware of the silences. Because the musical time-beat in words and phrases affects their meaning just as the fast or slow beats of the human heart affects the way we say things or even what we say. Or course this listening can be overdone. Writing can become too consciously balanced. In other words it may need some rougher treatment, to be knocked around a bit as some of our modern writers have done.

And of course writing means watching as well as listening. A preface to a collection of works by the French writer Colette says:

If her autobiography has any story it is that of a born watcher. Her view of life was austere, unsentimental, even harsh. She knew that sooner or later we would lose the innocence we were born with and that therefore we can only glimpse it from afar in children and in the pre-human kingdom we call animal, vegetable and mineral. She said about writing: "Only describe what you have seen. Look long and hard at the things that please you, even longer and harder at the things that cause you pain. Set no store by the unusual expression, beware of embellishments and obvious attempts at poetry."

I think on the whole writers tend to feel the need to move around a bit, perhaps because of the static and isolated nature of their work. They also have a fear of idleness – partly because of the slowness of writing. Here is Dickens writing from Switzerland to one of his publishers: "A week of idleness – idleness so rusting and devouring, so complete and unbroken." "You can hardly imagine", he goes on,

what infinite pains I take, what extraordinary difficulty I find in getting on *fast.* Invention seems the easiest thing in the world. But the difficulty of going at what I call a rapid pace is prodigious. It is almost an impossibility. I suppose this is partly the absence of city streets and numbers of figures. It seems as though they supplied something to my brain which it cannot bear to lose. For a week or a fortnight I can write in a retired place, yet a day in London sets me up again and starts me. But the toil and labour of writing without *that* magic lantern is immense! My figures seem to stagnate without crowds around them.

It's interesting that one of the ways Dickens was able to free himself from the immense pressures of his life and to think about his work was to go out alone at night into the streets and walk about for hours. And here is the opposite feeling expressed by V.S. Pritchett: "There is too much opinion in the cities." He compares this with being in the country where, he says: "One can let the bucket down into the subconscious."

I'm aware that I haven't said much about pleasures and pitfalls, far less how to write a short story. But the honest fact is that no one can really tell another how to write. I know, in part, why one writes. It is often because out of the chaos of a short life we may feel the need to make something more or less whole and complete, to gather up whatever vision or experience we may have had – whether it is of love, sorrow, disappointment, a sense of the ridiculous, the comic or tragic happenings in life – to gather these so that they are not totally lost.

Finally may I go back to the idea of the limited nature of the story and how we can use it. To speak about Flannery O'Connor again – she often wrote her stories about people severely limited, physically or mentally, or deformed by intolerance, self-righteousness and so on. But she didn't stop at more obvious limitations. She said that the basic experience of *everyone* is the experience of human limitation. This "human limitation" both tragic and comic is, it seems to me, what the writer makes it his business to express. And the greatest writers deliver us for a time from the frustrations and limitations of life. We are in some deep way calmed and set free. This has nothing to do with escapism. Perhaps this calm, this fullness, comes from experiencing in any work of art something which is, by its nature – and like the best story or novel – limited, yet also complete. I said we are made free for a time, yet not only for a time, after all. One of the best ways of resisting the chaos in us and around us is to get the habit of reading. In fact learning to read is the only way of learning to write. It is not a case of becoming obsessed with somebody's style and trying to copy it. Rather, it is being in the emotional company of books – being warmed, sustained, comforted, stimulated and made more courageous. And because life is short there is really only time to read the best – in other words that now rather maligned and laughed-at phrase Good Books. And what is a Good Book? How do we recognise it – or for that matter, a good story? It would be exceedingly snobbish to say it was *never* the popular best-seller or the moneymaking blockbuster. Nearer to the mark, however, might be Nabokov's definition in one of his essays – that we recognise good writing with "the mind, the brain, the top of the tingling spine." A major writer, he says, combines these three – a storyteller, teacher, enchanter – but it is the enchanter in him that predominates and makes him what he is. Luckily we can always recognise good books if we read widely and, thankfully, we can now stop talking about limits. The best is without limits. Even if we were to read every minute of our lives we should never come to the end of it.

If you ever wish to write and, like me, sometimes despair of putting words together, be comforted by that great French stylist, Flaubert, who himself once wrote in a letter: "Language is like a cracked kettle on which we beat out tunes for bears to dance to, when all the time we long to move the stars to pity."

The Cage

Elspeth Davie

When I was a young girl staying one holiday with my aunt and uncle I experienced a kind of horror when I discovered that an old woman a few doors away had expended all her love and every bit of warmth in her heart on a canary in a cage. This alarmed me. The fact that the bird was a captive made it worse. If she had loved some free creature that could have escaped the love at any moment, it would have seemed to me better. But the woman and the caged bird were tied up in a way that was disturbing. Sometimes when I went up and down the road to do shopping for my aunt I would see the owner of the bird poking some bit of food inside the bars or swinging the cage with the tip of her finger. When I mentioned to my aunt my peculiar unease I was told how extraordinarily unfeeling I was. Indeed she was shocked. One day she hoped I might learn to be kind. The woman, she explained, would be lonely and thankful to have the bird. The bird would simply be happy and thankful to have the food. Long ago it would have forgotten the ancient life of birds amongst leaves, trees and dangerous bigger birds that could tear others to death in one second.

I had known for a long time that I would never be really kind nor perhaps even perfectly human. Yet I knew what the thing was, of course, because both my aunt and uncle were genuinely kind, and even the friends of my own age seemed to have no difficulty in being generous and warm to one another.

As time went on I felt the inevitability in things. The once-wild bird, the lonely old woman and the unkind girl – these made up a trio that could now never be altered. Sometimes the three of them came into my dreams. Or were they nightmares: I was bewildered about the whole business of human feeling. Was it true, deep and endless, or questionable, expendable and short-lived?

The old woman died rather suddenly one day. In the draught of a darkened room the bird in its cage still swung, like a travesty of happiness, till relatives of its former owner came to take it away. For a while I felt a certain amount of self-hatred which swiftly changed to an early adolescent vanity. There was some talk of a happy place, presumably unknown to anyone, where the old woman had gone. "But not with the bird!" I exclaimed triumphantly. "Thank God it has escaped!"

"Try not to bring God into it", my aunt briskly replied.

The empty house was very quickly sold, but first I developed an obsession with its former inhabitant and then an interest in the new owner. He was a rather elderly man who worked most of the time in the garden. He often came to the fence when I passed and, leaning across to greet me, he would pull the heavy gardening gloves from his hands. Then he would draw each glove down over two separate spokes of the fence – a series of gestures indicating that he was perfectly prepared for a long talk. We had many conversations at the beginning of the summer and I was anxious that they should continue. At first, no doubt, it was a selfish and one-sided thing. I had many questions to ask him, but I was chiefly anxious to know what kind of creature I was myself. He had scarcely seen the former inhabitant of the house, and had spoken to her for only a few minutes. Now I felt impelled to talk to him about woman and bird.

"Did I have to love her because she was lonely and had only a bird to look after?" I asked.

"No, no," he replied, "you don't have to love people because of anything they are or do, or for what they have or don't have. You simply love them because you can't help it."

"But did I have to love that bird because it was in a cage?" I asked next.

"No," he said again, "that would be more like pity. Love and pity are different. And, besides, who knows, the bird had probably stepped out of the egg while in the pet-shop. Perhaps it had never known the sky, the trees or anything else."

Then I dared to ask him if I had to be disgusted with myself because I had no great feeling for the woman.

"Well," he said, "you can't use up all your feelings in one go, can you? You might need them for other things and people."

It soon became clear that my uncle and aunt were not happy that I should lean over gates speaking to absolute strangers about love, birds, pets, loneliness, self-disgust or anything else. In due course they, somehow or other – but politely and firmly – conveyed to this man that they were not pleased about these talks. As for myself, I took it that a long visit from a young girl was a great responsibility for them – something I would understand as I grew older.

From then on, I asked our neighbour fewer questions. He spent more and more time inside his house. Yet our talk did not totally stop. It simply became exceedingly polite, more strangely formal and unbelievably sad. This was the time when it dawned on me that few creatures were happy, neither birds, curious schoolgirls, old women, uncles and aunts, or newcomers to any district at all in the city.

One day, however, the man next door picked a tall, yellow rose for me and handed it over the fence without a word. I was proud to put it in a vase on my aunt's dining-room table that evening. "I am really, *really* sorry," said my aunt – and I knew she meant it – "but that must not happen again. Never. Of course we must always try to be helpful and as polite as possible. But your uncle and I know nothing about our neighbour yet. In fact, he has hardly spoken to either of us. Only to you. You have to know people a great deal better before you accept a flower or anything at all, for that matter."

When I looked into my mirror that night I saw that something had changed. They had given me the best bedroom – "spare" it was sometimes called. Behind me the white walls appeared to draw closer, their angles sharper. Within this safe enclosure I seemed different. I looked coolly alert. I looked knowing. And I was proud of it. I knew I might live for years and years, yet I was beginning to fade and die already. I did not mind.

From Elspeth Davie's Journal

Saturday, January 15th, 1939

A mighty wind tonight. L. and I were out fairly early before tea when it was not so strong, and the clouds were like great golden fishes against the pale evening sky. But later in the evening when we were out again the wind made one mad and terribly alive. Even to sit in front of the fire and listen to it was to become more and more restless to be out fighting with it and knowing its strength.

This time it was wonderfully clear, a full white moon and stars. Now the clouds were like long silver fish against the dark sky. More than ever tonight there is the sense of this living as a great race against Time and Eternity will the "wingèd chariots" close at one's back.

Especially this year I have had this sense of living against time, gasping against a great wind. Yet it is often a fallacy to call this immense struggle to keep one's head above water in so many things, living. The days when we truly live are days far more full of peace, more simple than this. But the struggle against the wind was tremendously refreshing. Having sung against it, shouted against it, run against it, defeated it and been defeated by it, one could at last settle with a kind of peace by the fire again.

Sunday, January 23rd

It seems absurd to suppose that a really good person should be necessarily happy, for no person, whatever his qualities and much less if he is at all sensitive, could ever or perhaps has no right to be happy in this world. But I think those whom we call good have an inner peace which though not happiness itself, is akin to it, a place, which to the wanderers seems a wonderful and almost impossibly difficult thing to find. Yet I think that though it comes along through much dust and years, it comes not through a great striving, and panting after it and forcing oneself on, but rather through some kind of other defeat, a complete humility of all one's self. And, by God, that is a difficult thing indeed. Only when one has it can one be said truly to live. How can one sing whilst still struggling to breathe.

Sunday, April 3rd

This day's silence makes one think a bit about the significance or insignificance of words. I think it is often the case that those who appear to have the most perfect self-assurance and confidence, always knowing the exact right thing to say and when to say it, leaving no moment for silence to become marked, those people may be often very far from self-assured, perhaps even very shy. Only when company, or maybe two people, are absolutely at their ease, is silence a welcome guest, becoming as beautifully expressive as any words can be. Shyness certainly seems to take some very varied opposing forms – sometimes intense silence, sometimes perfect poise of speech, too flawless for ease. Breaking the long silence of a shy person is a mighty undertaking. One feels that the words which break such a silence must be pretty stupendous ones for they must shatter the silence of eternity itself. Usually they are the most facetious ever uttered.

Sunday, April 10

Real tragedy is, I think, not something which shocks. One takes it often in quietness through impotence to help in some cases, and often merely because one recognises this vein of tragedy to be always through life; it is a part of life and as such can be accepted with the other parts.

In the last few days I have seen two women weeping and another has spoken quite simply of something which has hurt her life pretty badly from early days. Because I have lived in certain circumstances which give one years of understanding, I can see how tragedy is often the simplest of emotions, because more intense.

The way a man walks upstairs, a woman staring out of a window, a few perfectly simple words, silences – these may be the very actions of tragedy itself. One comes to see that bitterness never did help nor ever will help anyone and that to suffer without bitterness is one of the greatest things a person can show to a world which, God knows, cries out for comfort and healing.

Monday, July 11th

...Our three days walking [in the border country] was worth it even for the looking back, for the odd funny incidents and people you can share the memory of afterwards. However the last night and day after were the most interesting for me. We made our soup and salmon and I cut bread and fell to talking to one sitting in front of the fire, a dark, heavy sort of a fellow at first sight, dark brooding eyes behind glasses, an ancient brown polo jumper and dirty suit. He mentioned Edinburgh and the Phil. class; we started off about the subject and I clean forgot the bread and everyone else. He is a person with whom one gets right down to things at once – a great rest and joy, this. Supper brought the discussion to a close for a while until the others were washed up and he came wandering out into the scullery, and we took up the talk again standing by the window. We went at it at first hammer and tongs – both hungering to talk and discuss real things. I have rarely met anyone who talks so intensely or listens so intensely, taking a look at you now and then, encouraging you with a 'yes?' now and then, waiting and staring out of the window. To get in a word I had often to stop this great flood of talk, interrupting for a moment, he suffering this with patience. In our talk, we introduced ourselves and a half-suspicion was confirmed when he gives his name George Davie, whom I have often heard spoken of. He took Honours Classics and Phil, taking a scholarship to Germany last year, and now going in to Drever's post in 1st Ordinary this year, lecturing and tutoring – an extraordinary interesting mind and a great talker – the Dr. Johnson of Varsity as he is called. We discussed then most things under the sun and many beyond it – mostly philosophy – a slow, deep-sounding voice...

After breakfast Davie and I talked steadily on until dinner and in the end had the room to ourselves and buckled to with a vengeance. This first intense hunger to talk had burned itself away; it was a pleasanter, more deeply satisfying talk. There is extraordinary satisfaction in this, conversation mounting swiftly like two winged things each sweeping the other higher, each seeing a broader view of things at every movement. Talked mostly of books and art, social work. This is what I need more than many things just now, and it is perhaps what one misses most even in Varsity where one should get it. There are few people who seem to care to get down to things or to find great joy in discovering or discussing... After dinner we went down to the P.O. for stores and to see the other two off; packed up our things and sat in the window room reading in the sun until Davie came out and sat between at the table talking again ten to the dozen for long intervals, then sitting silent, heavy; the kind of person one would say seeing him suddenly that he was either clever or a clod. He has a rather rare, delightful smile like a little boy; he smiled suddenly up at Morag, bit his nail, and was lost with wonder at nothing. An interesting soul to watch...

I found our talks a great comfort and encouragement. When I came away I felt sore and impotent; I wanted to come down to things, to listen and talk about real things, to meet people on what they are really interested in, somehow to break through and find ground somewhere. Also the whole business of careers and writing, being of any service in clearing away some of this almighty chaos. On all these things we talked, and much of it was well said. I felt we could, in the end, have spoken about anything – a rather blessed feeling. We said goodbye, and Morag and I bundled in the back of the car with knapsacks and sticks and shoes and other unknown people. Davie stood rather dirty and awkward, waving us off. He reminds me rather of some animal staring lost, through a wilderness, yet discovering light; somehow weighing himself and everything else down to something solid and basic in his search for it. He has the intensity of the true philosopher and artist; I have seen something of it in others who think, Donald Mackinnon for one. I am happy that we met. I believe we rather liked each other.

Tuesday, September 20th

I have spent the last week in Glasgow, shopping, visiting, listening in, visiting the Exhibition, seeing a picture, drinking tea, with cigarettes by the fire in pyjamas at midnight, talking, reading. So life goes on in a week of world crisis. All the time at odd moments during the day we got news of the Czechoslovakian situation. One evening coming out of a picture we stepped, still dazed, into the crowded street; round lamp-posts people were reading black headlined newspapers, whilst strangers peered over their shoulder; everywhere bunches of anxious persons. Yet over everything there was a kind of brilliance, a sort of false gaiety born out of impotence and a sense of finality, the agony of things finishing before they are begun. Churches were to be open in the early part of this week

14

for prayers. This is the most natural thing in the world with some people and possibly often brings out much of the finest in people, but it is strange to think that if war, which would involve our country, is averted, there will be a general thank-God cry and a feeling that prayers have been answered – the prayers for peace. But what peace? The peace of Great Britain, perhaps. But what of China and Japan, Spain, the Jewish persecution, social war, cruelty between individuals. The prayer must surely be for a greater, deeper peace than we as human beings can understand. It seems to me that all true peace comes through some terrific defeat. Only out of such defeat it would seem some ultimate victory comes.

Sunday, November 20th

On Friday evening I saw *Othello* with Donald Wolfitt taking the leading part. It was really wonderfully well done. A tremendous play, with bits of it almost too great to bear. In the intervals we passed peppermints and chattered cheerily about little things. I wonder if it is because we can't suffer the pain of reality for too long periods at a time. Certainly such a play seems to be one of the real things in an unreal world.

One sometimes talks of coming down to reality, after hearing a great piece of music or some play, but it is surely the other way round. So often it is one's ordinary life which is unreal and small. In great Art one comes to grips with what is really true and it seems unnecessary to applaud or praise, and there are no words left. The silence in recognition of greatness is the silence of people looking at stars or mountains.

The Mime

Elspeth Davie

Adam had been trained in both dancing and mime, but it was as a mimic that he first made his name. He could mimic anything in the natural world. He could show how a fierce bird could fly up and fall on its prey from a great height with sharp, outstretched claws. This was all rather strange because he didn't look particularly strong or agile; physically he was not impressive. But it was not only birds. He could mimic animals. He could show how a sleek leopard slid softly out of the undergrowth at midnight. No one could understand how he did this. Some swore to God his leopard had fierce, yellow eyes whereas, in actual fact, Adam's eyes were a soft grey and expressed only a mild surprise at the impact his performance caused.

Naturally, he could play all the many varieties of monkey – eating, playing, scratching, scrambling about the branches. But that would be easy enough, said his audience. Anyone could manage that. Aren't they the closest thing to human beings? Unfortunately, such words often brought up an angry argument about the Origin of Man which could become very heated – leading down into the depths of the squealing, fetid jungle right up to an angel-filled heaven. The mime could also bring off, without effort, a rather eerie interpretation of the sun going down and the moon appearing through dark clouds.

"Oh, how ridiculous!" someone cried at the idea. "One can do movement obviously, but not darkness and light. It's madness to talk that way!"

True enough, there was a kind of craziness about Adam. He could show the wind frightening flocks of birds and twisting leaves and flowers. His interpretation of insects was not so attractive, people agreed, because insects were difficult to love, especially when munching parts of other insects. Butterflies were different, of course, allied as they were to flowers, colours, perfume and sunshine. But Adam demonstrated both grotesque insects and delicate butterflies as if showing two sides of every living thing. Horrors were never far from beauties, nor beauties from the horrors.

This made some people wonder about his humanity. On stage it was absolutely impossible to imagine him as husband, father, an uncle or even a son. He appeared to have no personality or covering of his own as he changed swiftly from reptile's scale to bird's feather, from monkey fur to insect brittleness, from brittleness to frailty. He had no long-term identity at all.

"There must be some way of getting at him –" they said, "of getting at him by the hair, of tugging that fake monkey fur, or catching him by those tail feathers, disjointing one of his insect legs."

"No, he must be helped to become *human*", said one.

"He'd better go to a clever doctor," said another, "the kind who understands the importance of being a man – a proper man rather than all those creatures he was never meant to be."

Adam took the hint and went to a very clever doctor. They talked for hours and hours together about the difference between men and monkeys, between men and leopards, between men and birds, insects and fragile butterflies. Lastly, the young man was made to understand, once and for all, that there was no connection whatever, and never had been, between his face and the moon's face, between his smooth brown head and the sun's flaming orb. The young man listened carefully as to why he must not try to be anything other than an ordinary man. It was foolish to try and would eventually make him very unhappy indeed. The good news was that there was still a very wide, interesting choice for him. He could still be a faithful, hard-working husband, a wise father, in time a kind old grandfather, and always – even before these possibilities came up – a good and trusted friend.

The doctor made an excellent job of Adam. The stage was not entirely forbidden, and one day he found himself on the boards again in front of a large audience. He was not certain now exactly what was expected of him. In fact he was not sure of anything any more. He flapped his hands for a time. He moved his elbows and tried to preen invisible feathers, but there was no way he could now resemble a bird. The sleek leopard coming out of the jungle with its luminous yellow eyes seemed so far back in the past that he might as well have attempted a tabby cat sitting against a garden wall. For a moment he sat on the empty stage like a nervous amateur while the audience waited even for a monkey. For surely monkeys were as easy to imitate as one's own relatives. Anyone could do monkeys in his own home.

However, after a while, seeing nothing for their money, people grew restive. Once it had seemed this man had the essence of living creatures within himself. Now he had lost it. He was obviously just like themselves and that was all there was to it.

"He is nothing!" they exclaimed. From the best seats in front of the house some men began to throw things – nothing dangerous, but nevertheless humiliating – caps, rolled-up newspapers, some small, hard parcels and a ball of string. Adam attempted an intricate act with the string but succeeded simply in tying his own hands together. Mocking laughter followed this clumsiness. The women used anything they could find in their handbags – one throwing a twist of boiled sweets at his head, and another a hard little compact which opened, emitting a fine shower of white powder on his hair. This, along with his drawn and startled face, managed, in seconds, to age him curiously.

"We paid money for good seats – and all for nothing!" one called out and the seats clacked back as they started to leave the theatre for trains and buses into the suburbs. Soon they were all gone.

Adam sat down, cross-legged, and stared into the empty space before him. Lights were being clicked off all round the building. First the white curve of the highest balcony grew dark, and then the two below. Soon only a faint shimmer came from the place where white plaster nymphs on tiptoe held up the gilded wreaths at either side of the darkened boxes. Finally, the bright spotlight that had illumined his own head vanished, taking away, at one stroke, his persona. The young mime was bewildered. Who or what was he: Animal, bird or human being? Dancer or mimic? Or simply a ghost shining with its own dim light? What was this place anyway? Only a vast building of curved, empty shells and black boxes from which even the echoes had receded. No doubt this was the end of his career.

Suddenly, from far off, he heard the click of heels – loud in the polished corridor outside the auditorium, but soon growing soft as they approached him up the carpeting of the central aisle. Adam moved from the front of the stage and crouched down in case some other missile should come hurtling through the air. A very young girl with a sheaf of programmes on her arm was staring up at him. She laid the papers down and placed both hands flat on the dusty stage.

"Oh, please don't stamp on my hands!" she exclaimed.

"Why ever should I do that?" Adam replied.

"I've heard you can be cruel", she said. "I've often watched your act myself. You can be a leopard, a malicious monkey and a fierce bird of prey."

"Well, that's all in the past now", said Adam. "Tonight I came to the end of my repertoire. I could see from the look of their backs that they're not coming here again. The mothers were taking their children away, telling them not to bother looking round. Husbands and wives were leaving hand in hand – couples who'd never joined hands for years and years."

"That means we're both free now. I've been waiting to leave myself for months", said the usherette, taking a single programme from her sheaf and tearing it up. Adam felt a mild misgiving in his heart as the white scraps fell between them like confetti. "I've watched your performance often enough," she went on, "and I can tell you what's gone wrong. The difficulty is that everlasting, all-animal act. People like animals, of course, but they like to imagine how other persons get on as well. They want something human to identify with. They'd like to feel their experiences are being looked at and most of all their successes. They don't want to see only birds and leopards. Not even butterflies. Tell the management you must have a break for a bit. Doctor's orders. In the interval think about other ways of getting across. You're a dancer as well as a mime. Start with your triumphs and successes, moving on to joy. Dance joy then! Dance happiness!"

So Adam made a determined shot at dancing happiness. But it wasn't as easy as he had imagined. However, having played the monkey and the leopard, he was practised in high leaps. He soon discovered, however, that simply leaving the ground was not all there was to it. He tried to dance the joy of any triumph he'd had in life – and drew a blank. He danced the tearing open of long letters supposedly crammed with promises and good news, yet clearly destined for the wastepaper basket. He threw up sham banknotes and shiny tin coins into the air to show his luck in business. His luck in love was simply a mix of bright headscarves and handkerchiefs from many countries, scarves which he snatched unexpectedly from his sleeve to show he had danced with girls from every part of the world. He showed how free and happy life could be if only one went about it in the right way as he claimed to have done himself – forever leaping high and circling this stage on his toes and finally demonstrating how one might reach every place and person one desired in life by simply turning a series of graceful cartwheels from one end of the footlights to the other.

When he came to the end of this act there was a slight pause, and then a little half-hearted clapping. Although his audience stayed in their seats, he had a keen ear for the faint applause and knew exactly what it meant.

"You were quite wrong to imagine I could dance joy", he said to his girl who was waiting in the wings. "It has never been my strong point, and evidently not theirs either. I only wish I'd stayed with my leopard, my monkeys and my butterflies who don't show in public how happy or unhappy they are or even how beautiful or how ugly. I might have learned something about myself into the bargain. But I'll do better in the next half. There'll be no inkling of joy there. I shall show them the inexplicable bad luck of most human beings – all, I might have said, but that would be pushing it a bit. Anyway, I'll show them something more realistic and recognisable this time!"

As Adam's life had not been one of the easiest he was very well fitted to play the part of deeply disappointed persons who had waited long in the line but missed the best jobs, who had been thrown out of lodgings and fallen out with friends, who had been wanderers in great cities and tramps throughout the countryside. He needed few props in the city scenes – a bed, a table, a window-frame, a mirror on one wall. He allowed his audience a few moments to remember this lumpy bed, the ink-stained table and flyblown mirror before he entered silently in darkness and flung himself down to sleep. After long silence and when a blue, morning light had pierced the keyhole, he slowly danced and dragged himself out of bed and went to the mirror. Exactly what he saw there nobody could be certain. Sometimes he seemed to see his face as something better than he'd expected, more often something worse and promising worse to come. Again, what he saw as he crossed to the window and stared up and down the street was a total mystery to most. How could the approach of an innocent milkvan, the friendly postman and, above all, a group of cheerful children crossing the road cause him such pain, such sorrow, even terror? And why take the audience with him to these outlandish lookouts? Was this called entertainment?

But occasionally, even before the lights came on, Adam could sense the reluctant relief of recognition in his unseen audience – the quietness of people staring at their world, loving and hating what they saw, looking forward to the future but at the same time dreading it; wanting everything, losing everything; picking it all up again; starting again for the umpteenth time.

It was not long before Adam's girl told him she could no longer stay with him. "So you've found your audience at last", she said. "They seemed perfectly pleased to see their happiness and misery played about with. Well, that's not for me. I like things to be straightforward. I shall find a perfectly simple man who knows who and what he is, and I shall make him happy." She was rather a tall girl. He noticed, after she kissed him, that she went on staring abstractedly over his shoulder as if searching for this simple man who knew who and what he was. Adam didn't resent this. He had never known in the past, didn't know now, and never expected to know at any time in the future, who or what he was. Or why. Nevertheless, he hung around for a bit in case the ideal should turn up.

This man, she'd said, would be a tower of strength – a leaning tower, for the time being, while still needing her support. His character, however, would be already plain. He would be confident but not conceited, creative but not crazy, artistic but not arty, light-hearted but not flighty, witty but not flippant. She searched the seats through a pair of strong binoculars even as she described him, assuring Adam that such a man must undoubtedly be in the audience somewhere. It could only be, she added, that a sudden dimming of lights after the final curtain, plus a blinding floodlight on stage, had made him – for the moment – a little difficult to spot.

A Universe of one's own?
Elspeth Davie and the narrative of the "gap"
Marina Spunta

The world of Elspeth Davie is compact, self-contained, like the environment of *The Night of the Funny Hats*, the story which gives the title to her third collection, where "the place existed for itself". To go deeper into this world I will adopt the same pattern the author uses to portray it and look at it from her own point of view. As she states in *Beyond the Words*, the collection of stories edited by Giles Gordon, the writers who chiefly interest her are "those who strike at an angle to experience" and this she does herself by conveying the absurdity of a day-to-day reality through a seemingly simple form. To present Elspeth Davie's vision of reality, which can be summarized by the key-word "gap", I will first focus my attention on the "author's voice" as she speaks in the few published interviews and in the ones I was kindly granted in winter 1991.

What Davie notices in everyday life, what confirms the peculiarity of her vision, is the "strange, the desolating, the ludicrous" (*Writers in Brief* 2). Her stories, despite their apparently common setting portraying the "day-to-day experience", are always extraordinary because of a weird touch, which makes characters and things unnatural, at times fantastic. The portrait she gives of modern society is based on the coexistence of two opposite and contrasting realities: the "things" that everybody is aware of and the "hidden", ultimate reality that only particular characters can grasp. The unperceived interplay of these two levels creates the irrational, the strange, the ludicrous, since the reality-principle is constantly violated by upside-down norms. The essence of human society is therefore chaos, alienation and illness, as opposed to Davie's ideal order that is "whole" and "healthy". Thus "gap" and "paradox", as a broader synonym for absurdity, can be taken as the key concept underlying her writing.

In this world of chaos and voids the writer, and the artist in general, as someone still capable of imagination, is one who can fill the "gap", the existential "blank" of modern society. This is Davie's idea of the writer's work as stated in Gordon's *Beyond the words*:

> Part of his business as a writer, in an age of form-filling and labelling, curt questions and short answers, is to see that the silent uniqueness of persons and situations, their essence if you like, doesn't get lost among files. It's his job to recognize and preserve the most secret side of life.

Her purpose in writing is even clearer in this extract from the interview she granted to me, where she insists on the "mission" of the writer:

> Every writer tries to bring out what is in, to illumine darkness and this could be a help to some people... Writers should express what they feel others are, talk other people's silences; they should be able to express things people find hard to tell, to grant them a kind of relief (ED)[1]

---

1. (ED) stands for my interviews with Elspeth Davie

The role of the artist in illumining darkness recalls the Romantic idea together with her conviction that

> Artists have had a good deal of disturbance that made them need to write and perhaps this is what has made them into artists... Often they have a disturbance they would like somehow to heal, to make into a whole, and a whole means healthy... But first they have to have this rather disturbing feeling about something they try to get into a whole composition. (ED)

In these words the basic duality of her thought emerges continually, between the existing "chaos" and the ideal "wholeness" she strives to achieve through her writing. Her prose is the very clever result of a difficult balance between two opposites: the "real" world and the "metaphysical" one; a chaotic matter and the ideal form; a wild imagination and an extremely precise and refined style, beside the constant question of involvement and detachment on the writer's part.

The "metaphysical" world, the "hidden" reality, can be achieved only through the power of imagination. Davie has a high concept of it, following the Romantic idea:

> It is a kind of instinct, a kind of spark that mixes itself with a sort of sympathy or a feeling of dislike you have for something. (ED)

Thus her preference for short-story writing, where her "flashing" imagination and her technique of building extremely detailed pictures are at their best. The importance of imagination is in its being "a different way of looking at reality, maybe the right one since there is so much strangeness and mystery in the world..." (ED), or, as Flannery O'Connor puts it:

> Imagination is a distortion of truth, but you may have to use a sort of distortion to get at the truth.

Despite her high concept of imagination, at the same time Davie feels the need to moderate it in order to create a "form", as

> The writing has to have some fairly reasonable form however much you want to write of chaotic things... even chaos must have some form, some style to make it readable. I do not mean that it is the same with every writer... American writers are a bit like that, they can be terribly violent, stormy... (ED)

and, asked for a possible reason for the apparent simplicity of her style, Davie answers that it is "just probably as it comes, perhaps it is easier for the writer" (ED) to have an ordered form.

> I think style has to do with character... Some writers are clear on the surface, what is called a simple style, yet it is probably made up of a great deal of complexity and struggle and chaos sometimes. (ED)

On the matter of style she seems to be quite concerned, almost fearing that her style could be "too smooth at times, patterned or too cool."(ED) At the same time her fear is that

> sometimes I might sound slightly inhuman, distant... Maybe I myself am not near enough... It is very difficult, a balance between expressing a tremendous lot of emotions and also having a certain amount of reserve. [Yet] I think you have to have this detachment. I am not sure how it works but you cannot get too emotionally involved (ED)

It now becomes easier to understand that, since "style has to do with character" (ED), her clear preference for a simple form to order the struggle underneath is the exact correspondent of her predilection for a reserved stance, to convey the violent feelings that originate a work of art. Davie seems quite a reserved person and writer, as she says herself:

> I do not think I am terribly outgoing. I think I can do it in writing as it is easier there." Yet "I don't like to write very much about myself... I do not think that my writing is autobiographical; if it were so I'd feel slightly embarrassed because I would go into family things and this is rather painful. (ED)

Yet she is aware that "only good writers let themselves go completely" and that "all writers have to feel free, and most of them do it, otherwise they will never write anything interesting".

The artistic detachment, which to her is a source of so many scruples, does not prevent her from a close observation of the object of art. As a former art student she is capable of acutely discerning reality, and this enables her to go beyond it, as she states:

> I rather tend to a detailed kind of writing because I enjoyed painting which is detailed. To write well you have to use your eyes, perhaps every sense. (ED)

Her unique ability to look at single objects that in her narrative often become symbols, is what gives her writing a visionary quality, unifying two opposite styles, realism and surrealism. While bridging the "gap" between these two contrasting modes, which are made into a whole in her stories, she creates masterly portrayals of the void she sees in modern society and the lack of identity of contemporary people.

The "gap", as the key word of Davie's narrative, is the constant feature in her vision of reality. It is soon evident that the society she describes in her stories is not a real community, for its main character is separation. Actually, Elspeth Davie does not seem so interested in the whole society as she is in observing single persons. Yet, while acutely depicting the single egos who populate her stories, she gives a striking portrait of present-day society as nothing but a conglomerate of egotistic entities which hardly ever come together.

The most recurrent feature of these individuals is their loneliness – of which, however, we find different manifestations, depending on the characters' different reactions to it. The majority of Davie's characters are utterly lonely in the sense that they have no personal link with others. Many are widows or widowers, while married people are exceptions. The widowed condition, another variation of the basic idea of the "gap", seems to be chosen as an emblematic state of solitude and disillusionment about love and life, while at the same time suggesting the real essence of married life, that is seen, paradoxically, as one of separation.

It is agreed that "she is particularly good on lonely people, isolated by their own peculiarities" and her first striking achievement in this direction is *The Spark*. The unnaturalness of the characters in these stories is one of the reasons for their alienation from the rest of the world, their obsessions setting them awkwardly in relationship with other people and the environment.

One of the best characters in the first collection is undoubtedly the protagonist of 'A Woman of Substance'. This woman is the epitome of isolation and the need to conform, in order to hide her loneliness and dissatisfaction with herself. In this passage we can appreciate Davie's subtle psychological analysis, acutely bringing to light the dark corners of a disturbed, lonely person.

> Miss Read had one day found herself suddenly and absolutely on her own. All the same, she treated any chance remark or question about this as a great indelicacy on the part of the questioner – something she might still prevent by turning her head sharply aside, smiling as at some flippant remark, or simply pretending not to hear at all. In this way she felt she had averted some danger which had come too close, and might in the end threaten her whole existence.

Other deep analyses of split identities are those stories centred on "neurotic" characters who are affected by obsessive-compulsive disorders. The most striking and powerful example is 'Family House', a story in the first collection, where the atmosphere of oppression is brilliantly rendered from the start by the analysis of objects which have "taken over" people who live with the compulsive thought of serving the house's needs.

Another common theme in Davie's stories, related to the motif of the mask and of loneliness, is the difficulty of verbal communication, again a variation of the basic keynote of "gap". She examines the absence of communication in its different degrees, starting from complete silence and ending with pretended communication, its causes and consequences, while at the same time stressing the underlying longing for oral exchange.

Silence is only one clear metaphor of the "gap", the most striking sign of breakdown of communication, which recurs in her stories. Indeed we find a series of appalling silences and understatements that point out the impossibility of communicating one's experience and of having interpersonal relationships. A paradoxical example is 'The Return' (in *A Traveller's Room*) where the initial "prolonged silence in the room one evening after supper" is maintained until the climax, with the mother's "return" to the water – she was a mermaid – that implies the impossibility to communicate within the family and, first, within the couple.

Another barrier for communication lies in the structure of the stories, based on pairs of opposing characters speaking different languages, a sort of dumb conversation in which each character cannot acquaint the other with their own sensations. Davie's characters are split, like all her world, into two contrasting positions: on the one hand those who are trapped into the chaotic, irrational and void reality or in their obsessive selves, on the other hand those who are granted the power to "see" things in their real dimension and to read beyond the appearance of reality. These "spark-characters", a definition I take from the title of her first collection, are of course outsiders, out of step with a conforming society and therefore the only ones capable of "illuminations of truth". Significantly, children are the majority in this group, besides artists and a few sick persons and travellers, all of whom are distinguished by a striking power of imagination.

Children are almost the only characters in contact with nature, still capable of innocence and generosity. As complementary protagonists their role is to try to unify the split reality – though their attempt is usually in vain. In a world of absurdity, they become the only "whole" individuals by rejecting a reality that is for them only a means, a sign of a deeper world. Their outstanding imagination, like the artists', enables them to reach this deeper reality and make the world a "bearable place to live in".

An example of a "spark-character" is the girl in 'A Traveller's Room' who, while looking over the things left by the room's usual resident

> felt a premonition of some sadness in another person – not a sharp, pene-
> trating sadness, but the slow, enveloping kind that folds in forever to keep
> out air and light.

Despite children's attempts to heal adults' isolation, their illuminations are always disregarded by the older characters who are, paradoxically, less mature. Only children in fact can experience visions of truth, like Caroline in 'Out of Season':

> Love, I saw in a flash, had nothing to do with the garland of roses or the
> blurred outline, but with absolute clearness of sight, a knife-sharp awareness
> of beginnings and ends.

The few gifted artists are, as usual, out-of-step persons who do not conform with the kind of art approved by society. A street-painter in 'Change of Face' is the only one who listens to the sorrow of a man (who has just lost his son) and who is incapable of rendering the man's grief except through a creation of imagination. Likewise the protagonist of 'The Sign-Painter', who is confined to a ladder, like the street-painter in his shelter, can look at the world from a different angle, detaching himself from the chaos underneath.

The striving for a unity, in the attempt to heal the "gap", is the key concept even when we come to the question of style. Paradoxically it is through a synthesis of opposite styles, realism and surrealism, that Davie achieves her aim to "make things into a whole". Starting from a realist point of view, she ends in a surrealist-symbolist mode through an unbroken process as the last code "springs" naturally from the first one. Her aim of precisely looking at reality as a means of discovering the "hidden" layer, takes her realism to the extreme of naturalism, appearing to watch her world from above, and, at the same time, of impressionism, as reality becomes a series of flashes in this insisted visual process.

This passage in the story 'Accompanists' is a powerful illustration of the author's "miniaturist work" on characters:

> An absolute silence falls and a short burst of clapping as the accompanists
> unobtrusively take their seats again after the interval. There is some time to
> study them before the singer himself comes back to the platform. The audi-
> ence stares fixedly at the two women. The young girl who turns pages is
> wearing a black blouse and a black silk skirt. She is slim, pale, with straight
> hair swept back from the forehead. Once she is seated they are aware of her
> startlingly straight back. She waits, modest yet confident, thin fingers clasped
> on her lap, her head already slightly inclined towards the piano. The pianist
> – a more formidable woman – waits, her feet firmly planted, strong hands

spread out on her knees and her head bowed. She is in black to the ankles. These two wait patiently, unmoving as images.

On the one hand, it is evident how realism is stretched into a naturalist technique, through the author's analysis of these passive characters, these "unmoving images", and, at the same time, into an impressionist technique, the description following the audience's perception of the scene as a series of glimpses. On the other hand, the persistent observation causes the internal metamorphosis of reality into surreality, as the details become unrealistic in their disproportionately magnified importance. The pianist's "strong spread hands" with their "large, strong-boned fingers" become even more grotesque as they are "spread on the narrow lines of a pleated skirt".

'Concerto' is a similar slow-motion filming of the situation, filtered through the eyes of the audience, and thus made strange. The insisted realism of the inner description of chaotic nature is a direct consequence of Davie's "search" and of her conviction that "to write well you have to use your eyes, perhaps every sense."

Thus the insistence on colour, also a consequence of her experience as a painter. Like everything in her stories, colours take a symbolic stance. As opposed to them, with even more symbolic implications, we find recurrent "white patches", "blanks", "gaps". The emblematic potential of white colour is brilliantly summarized in 'Write on Me' (a story in the latest collection, *Death of a Doctor*), where "a small boy and his father" are confronted with "a large square of canvas covered with a smooth, thick coating of pure, white paint."

> The expanse of white paint was curiously seductive. Enclosed by its broad frame, it gave, to some, a sense of total peace and safety. Not everyone felt safe, however. Some felt that if they stood too long staring, they might lose their voice, miss the meaning of the thing – if it had a meaning – and, at worst, fall through pure whiteness into space and lose their identity forever. The boy's father also felt this as he stared silently at the square, momentarily pet-rified, as if vainly searching for himself.

Symptomatically, only the small boy can spot the three words in a corner – "write on me" – to which he answers "I love this", for

> he was still rather sensitive about words and white spaces – how they looked and what they meant.

The symbolism of colours can be taken as the epitome of her style, as it unifies in itself the character of realist, impressionist, and surrealist descriptions. Symbolism, in fact, is another key word of Davie's narrative, making the split world into a double-faced unity. Her definition of symbols as "something that illumines the Truth, but at a rather difficult angle" recalls the one she gives of imagination, and links the concept of symbol with the one of "flash", both sharing the character of irrational "illumination". In her interview with Allan Massie she states: "Symbols? Well, I see them after I have done them."

Davie's insistence on "hidden" meanings sometimes risks exhausting the symbols, spoiling the "pleasure of the text" to be experienced in reading between the lines. In some places, in fact, the author tends to explain them, thus breaking their intrinsic power of "magic" implication. In those few cases in which they turn to open allegories, the tone of the stories moves into a sort of didacticism, at odds with her brilliantly balanced style. The urgency of the message, in fact, sometimes betrays the constant implicit moral, and her subtle, controlled form ends occasionally in abstract conversations, "strangely untuned dialogues" (Alan Spence).

In Davie's stories surrealism unexpectedly "springs" from within an apparently realistic, common setting – just as the unbound imagination of a "spark-character" suddenly and completely discards the rigid world of the other protagonists. The story 'Green Head' can be taken as an example of these epiphanies in a "common" reality, as the sudden growth of flowers on Ewan's head is comically pointed out by a painter with these words: "There is a surrealist something about it."

This grotesque sprouting suggests Kafkaesque metamorphosis, the absurdity of the situation being increased by a naturalistic, matter-of-fact style, an intrinsic characteristic of "magic realism", as defined by Chanady.

> Not long after the young man, Ewan, had turned eighteen years of age, he was astounded and ashamed one day to find spikes of new green grass beginning to grow in among the hair of his head.

Even in the "common" stories the readers are clearly invited to a "suspension of disbelief" as they are forced to abandon conventional reality to follow the characters and their obsessions. It is as if the situation were told from the point of view of the protagonist, who would present it in a candidly straightforward, always detailed way. If we look closer at Davie's stories we discover the accuracy of her narrative techniques, which are also based on the device of the "gap". It is worth stressing, first, the recurrence of physical "gaps" in the stories, alternatively in the form of "blanks", "breaches", "crevices", "holes", "cracks", "voids", and "spaces". These are clear symbols of the author's idea of an impossible completeness, owing to the all-pervading feature of division.

On a closer stylistic level, correspondingly, we discover a writing made of separate self-standing entities, just like the characters in Davie's world. This broken style is created by self-contained paragraphs, and, at the microtext level, by sentences which often stand by themselves, not necessarily linked to the preceding one, as they follow the characters' inner thoughts. Davie experiments with a "miniaturist" work of continuous collapses, since the explanatory links are usually omitted, as in the process of the mind. By suppressing more and more the "connective tissue" of the narrator's discourse, leaving only the essential, that is to say the characters' perceptions, her later stories achieve greater vividness and effectiveness.

As the central idea in Davie's writing, together with the paradox, the "gap" creates a new style that jettisons traditional forms. The narrative categories of space, time and plot are, in fact, void. When we come to the setting of the stories, we find that it is always vague, implied, contrasting with the extreme precision of description – conveying a sense of a symbolic setting. The time location is unimportant, if we consider the stories as "parables, all focusing upon moments of transition" (A. Kennedy). Given their abstraction, they seem meant to convey a message beyond time. The "gap" is again the basic technique. I have already mentioned the extent of silence in the stories. In the characters' conversations the "unsaid", the "implied" recurs, coherent with the picture of a split society. The irony in the lack of communication ends with the dissection of the medium of language itself, revealed as intrinsically ambiguous. An effective parody of the inadequacy of language to convey a meaning is often found in the titles, which tend to mislead the reader. Headings like 'A Woman of Substance', 'A Weight Problem', 'Change of Face', 'The Foothold', 'It is Your Turn', 'Geological Episode', 'Bulbs', 'Absolute Delight' or 'Waiting', effectively create suspense and confusion in the readers, as they imply their literal meaning. The reader is tricked by the existence of a double meaning the author is always keen on spotting, in a continuous interplay between real and abstract.

Another important tool, again based on the technique of the "gap", is rhythm. The necessary quick pace of the stories is managed through continuous "gaps", besides a wise choice of words, as the author says:

> In the short stories the rhythm is all important. You're always listening to it. It is true of course of anything, but a short story may stand or fall by it. It's a good deal of course like listening to a line of music – that's really why you often have to change words, because of the rhythm. It's a sort of instinctive thing. But you always know when it has gone wrong. (Allan Massie)

Besides rhythm, the essential component in Davie's writing is the imagery through which she hints at a deeper reality. As well as symbols, a great number of similes and metaphors build the compact structure of the stories, contributing to the atmosphere and implicit meaning.

In conclusion we can easily place Davie among the finest contemporary short-story writers. Her "subtly polished style" (Allan Massie) makes the chaos of the world into a "whole", through a form that is the synthesis of opposite codes and the renewing of traditional techniques, by means of the "gap", a direct consequence of her reticence.

The reason why she is not as widely known as her talent deserves is probably the "difficult" nature of her writing – her semi-surrealist style and her technique of "dissimulation". The first impression her stories make on the reader is that of oddity, peculiarity, that could easily lead one to set Davie and her characters in a "universe of their own". Yet, after a first reading, the social relevance of her writing and her ironical comment on modern reality becomes evident. It is only after a deeper analysis, though, that the reader can see her strong link with a tradition of nineteenth century writing and with contemporary literature, Scottish and worldwide. Thus what Davie creates is not a world apart, but is indirectly yet deeply connected with a wide range of literary works. The stylistic achievements of Davie's stories have not been praised enough. She is worthy of far more attention as a master of short story writing.

John McInnes

A Death in the Family

Shock news, although prepared:
"It's a blessing, she's been spared
the suffering that cancer brings."
Requiem mass; one woman sings
aloud the hymns, most mime or mumble;
pall-bearers bear, a brother stumbles.
Swept silently through city streets –
boxed face, boxed body, impervious to rain that beats
on friends desirous of attending
(no flowers please) at this, the ending
of a life. Simulating grief can be a test
of stamina and nerves – they do their best.
I hear banalities, let strangers shake my hand;
can't comprehend, can't understand
the meaning of this day. Where is her soul?
We walk towards the narrow hole
and stand with numbered cards around
a muddy pit, and put my mother in the ground.

The Lost Boys

Do dead men make sin sacred?
Do graves glorify a war?
Ask the lost boys
lying stiffly to attention
with fleshless faces, no tongues,
and sockets with no eyes.
Wild voices cried: "Forward! Do not falter!
Freedom is your cause!"
Then Death whispered: "Lie still for ever
in these foreign fields; let maggots strip your jaws.
Lie still and listen to the noise:
they call you heroes, they call you the brave boys."
What price the name of hero? What price their piteous souls
who ran, for boys' own reasons, to lie in nameless holes.
And so they lie, the bones of boys,
deprived of life and love,
while men march to their memory
and Victory struts above.
With fife and drum they celebrate, and words that are too shrill
for sons and brothers long destroyed – and still
the voices speak of patriots, and freedom, and how the boys were brave;

as mud-filled skulls, and faceless teeth, lie grinning in their graves.
Age did not weary them nor the years condemn
and fathers', mothers', lovers' eyes never saw those boys again.
So celebrate the broken hearts and sanctify lost boys
who lie so still and know, too late, the reason for the noise.

Rab Fergusson's Spree

Fergusson's banes an Fergusson's brains
wur laid doon in Canongate Kirk
in a narra hoose that wis built wi'oot stanes
an nae licht fur tae see through the mirk.
But Robert's nae chump, while he waits the last trump
he keeks oot, his neebors tae see –
or if 'is mooth's dry, wi an unco jump
he'll lowp fae the grave fur a spree.
For it's very well known, when you live on your own
yer ain company's gey hard tae thole –
it's surely nae fun tae reside all alone –
but it's worse. in the gun, in a hole.
Sae ilka dark nicht, it wad gie ye a fricht
tae see oor Rab saunterin oot;
e'en Aul' Reekie hersel's ne'er seen sic a sicht
as a ghaist, wearin haurdly a cloot!
He gied a keek (that's a glance that's oblique)
at his gravestane erected by Burns –
an stifled a tear at the words o his fiere
nae 'pompous lay' an nae 'storied urns'!
Then Fergusson stood as erect as he could,
tho' deceased, an a ruckle o banes
"Freen Rab ye wur right, tae expose an indict
'Enbrugh gentry' wha's hairts wur like stanes!
Their taste ran tae cairts, an Lucky Spence 'tairts' –
ne'er liftin their een tae Parnassus –
they only broke sweat when a hoor made them het
an gar'd them shoogle thur fat, titled arses!"
Ae nicht in July, he thocht he wad try
tae get inty a disco, ye ken –
sae he keekit up closes till he heard by an by
a helluva noise fae a pen.
Oor Rab gaed straight in, midst the clamour an din
an asked a young lassie tae dance –
the quine took a shine tae his dry, scaly skin
an decided she might tak a chance.
Her herr wis jet-black, an hung straight doon 'er back
wi some spiked oan the tap o 'er heid

but even a punk wad hae tae be drunk
tae dance wi a mannie that's deid!
The band started to play in the modern way
which seemed tae put Rab in fine fettle –
tho' jist oot 'is grave he started tae rave
wi this burd that jist loved Heavy Metal.
"D'ye like Grateful Deid?", she asked shakin 'er heid,
but Fergusson jist looked perplexed
"Well whit aboot thrash? or new-glam-punk trash?"
the revenant looked even more vexed.
No answer he gave, this thing from the grave
jist jigged lik a skinless Tom Jones
till the burd stared spellbound, shreiking over the sound
"Stripe me pink! ye kin see through 'is bones!"
The gyrating throng seemed to see nothing wrong
wi this skeleton, baring black teeth,
they'd seen mair frichtenin sights on Glesga Fair Nights
in the Working Men's Tavern in Leith!
But a bouncer ca'd Tam, wi a neck lik a ham
wha'd seen many a beer-sourin face
an wad let in a boar, or a pig thru the door
drew the line at deid bards wi nae face.
So Rab's foray for fun ended up on the grun
arse-up in a Royal Mile gutter
"If that wis a rave, ah'm better aff in the grave",
as he headed kirk-ward wi a mutter.
A mutterin ghaist wad arouse (in maist
toons) expressions o fear an alarm
but Embra noo contains sic a crew,
a ghaist is the *least* o the harm!
He crept in 'is crypt, (by Burns' cash equipped)
and silenced Clarinda's snide taunts
wi "You haud yer rammy! Burns musta been bammy
tae waant tae get inty *your* pants!"
Afore she could scour 'im, he'd pull't the earth ower 'im
wan last blink – then Silence Sublime.
He's fun oot wance again: Man must learn in PAIN
an HELL aye attends a 'guid time'!

Alistair Findlay

Fitba Cliché

(The Ba's no for Eatin)

I remember being told by Big MacIntyre
tae take mair time oan the ba'. Listen son, he says,
yir playin like the gress wis oan fire.
Yir blindin us aw wi the stour.

This is a gemm fur men,
no boays, or weans, or jessies.
If yir good enough, yir big enough, they say, but,
never listen or play tae the crowd,
an forget aw yir faither's advice,
an yir great uncle Tam's an aw,
wha played wi Champfleurie Violet's Cup Winning Team.
They days are aw gaun, like snaw aff
a Geordie Young clearance.

Then
it wis the people's gemm,
aw aboot the ba', an beatin yir men,
this way then that, then swingin it ower frae the wing,
an up like a bird tae heid it awa and intae the net.
The goalie, auld as yir faither an dressed like yir grannie,
stuck in the mud like a big stranded whale, Goal!
And a hundred thousand voices sang in Hampden Park.
Ye couldnae see the sun fur bunnets.

Romantic?
Ay, an aw for the glory o it.
Well, that's aw shite noo son,
the ba's no for eatin oanie mair.

Time was
when ye could tell a prospect
by the way he shed his hair,
or jouked bye his relations in the scullery,
but we still believed in Empire then,
ken,
when The Wee Blue Devils buried themselvs at the England end
and half o Europe, for a glory that wisnae worth haen,
oor ain, singin an deein like cattle,
brought hame not one lullabye in Gaelic.

> In the room the punters come and go
> Talking of De Stephano.

On the terraces,
beneath the stand,
a poet speaks for a nation:

the ref's a baam.

We,
whaur the comic and the cosmic meet,
an ambulance ball, a crowded street,
a psyche and a jersey steeped ower dark
b' the ruck, a people still, unique,
postmodern, post-Gramsci (*sic*),
manoeuvrin, multiform, and chic, ay missus,
chic as fuck.

SCOT-LAND! SCOT-LAND! SCOT-LAND!

Scotland,
Turn yir back tae the grandstand,
forget the suicide ba',
think mair o keepin possession,
Christ, frae some o yir ain side anaw!

Listen.
Ye cannae play fitba withoot the ba', okay?
An ye cannae govern yersel withoot a country,
even if ye are oan the committee.
(England taught us that)

Right then.

Play yir ain gemm,
afore the ba' eats us.

Again.

John Galt's 'Provost'

(With Explanatory Notes)

"their work... called Anglocentricity into question."
Robert Crawford, *Devolving English Literature*

When deacons, baillies, pawkies cleek
          (indignitaries sit cheek by cheek)
and glammer, and loot a sort a-jee,
          (to speechify, and brothers be)
n'outgait and blether in the causeys,
          (but keep they close in public ways)
thir hairs to lay upon the water,
          (by God, there's going to be a slaughter)

syne hooly, hooly, grippy me, the provost,
   (softly, softly, catchee monkey)
beeking in the lown of gelt,
   (basking in the calm of gold)
an ye rookit of every plack,
   (stripped bare of every penny)
quo he: "to rule without being felt".
   ("the great mystery of policy")

When deacons, baillies, pawkies cleek
an glammer, an loot a sort a-jee,
n'outgait and blether in the causeys,
thir hairs to lay upon the water,
syne hooly, hooly, grippy me, the provost,
beeking in the lown of gelt,
and ye rookit of every plack,
quo he: "to rule without being felt,
the great mystery of policy".

And see, no gabby prick-me-dainty bodie he, by gee,
(or talkative, pernickety person either) no, not he,
     by Christ,
     the Provost.

Jimmie MacGregor's Radio Programme On A Minor War Poet

Sing me no more sad-sounding roundelays
of death and war, of comradeship and gore,
of brotherhood's instinctive reaching to defend
each other until the very end, dear friend,
no matter whose, even your own.

For this disgrace, it is no less,
is a perversion of the deepest trace memories
we own, formed in the midst of every common birth.

Clutched and clutching we, gasping for air
through wetness and the blood, gripped
by overwhelming fear the powerful drive us to,
we know not where, or how, cracked into life
and passed around, clutched and clutching still,
till someone catches hold and we are held there,
fast and sure, unabandoned, ready to die or kill
for that same surety to remain, over and over
and over again.

Cats

Ann Lingard

The envelope merely stated: 'To the young lady who lives in the basement flat'. There was a single sheet of paper inside on which was written a poem in firm black ink. Catriona read it quickly, unable to take in the words.

> To *"The Lady-with-the-Sky-in-her-Hair"*
>
> Your black hair, glossy,
> Reaches out
> And entwines the blue sky,
> Wraps it in shining fingers
> And pulls it down
> Around your head,
> Like a blue, silk shawl.
>
> You are a celestial pillar,
> Rapt in beautiful, fierce anger,
> And even the cat
> Is cowed.

There was no signature. She read it again, and now she knew who had written it. She saw herself, raised high above the viewer's head, enhanced through his vision, and she was moved and excited. But she was also fearful, that he should interpret her in this way, and ensnare her.

As she folded the piece of paper, she saw another line of writing, on the back: *"What you need is a Tom!"* Even as she read this suggestion (or was it a proposition?), she thought she knew what was in the black plastic sack on which the envelope had been propped: and she was disgusted.

There was another dead cat in the lane. Catriona could just make out its shape where it lay stiffly in the mud. She hung her tights on the washing-line, leant against the railings and stared down into the lane behind the terrace. The lane was a dark, rutted gorge, its cobbles long since displaced and broken by heavy lorries and an endless sequence of men with road-drills, spades and inappropriate tarmac. It was bounded by stone walls pierced by wooden doors, some strong and locked like Catriona's, others broken and hanging. Behind the walls, their backgardens and dustbins rose even higher walls, four storeys high, of stern Victorian terraces.

The cat, once so large and vivid orange, was diminished and darkened by the surrounding stone. Would this corpse, too, suddenly vanish over-night? The terrace in which Catriona lived curved around the top of the hill, so that the windows and back door of her basement flat opened onto a steeply-sloping lawn. Her garden was small – the grass ragged, the few shrubs alive but stunted, the patch of soil that nourished nasturtiums and daffodils adequate but sooty – but she was happy to use it as an extension to her tiny flat. But it was a constant irritation that the neighbourhood cats used it, too. It was not only their noise that irritated (and sometimes in the night frightened) her: it was their casual acceptance that any patch of sun-light was theirs, that the dustbin and shrubs were parish boundaries to be sprayed with pungent stink, and the powdery soil had been provided as a public cats' convenience. The cats clawed open dustbin sacks, then sat and chewed, heads tilted, at stringy offal and kitchen towel soaked in miscellaneous juices; they formed small gangs that paced, with twitching tails, glaring at the opposition; and they hunted for newly-parked cars, searching out the warmest engine, stamping their muddy feet in triumph on the bonnet. Catriona hated them. She rapped on the window or opened the door and threw things. Once, she threw her shoe with such powerful anger that it sped the length of the garden and dropped over the railings out of sight. When she went to fetch it, treading cautiously down the steep, slimy steps towards the wooden door, the cat (amused and undeterred) peered down at her descending head, and purred.

There was so much food: not merely carelessly thrown junk, but purposely-placed food, offered by cat-owners and cat-less people who felt sorry for the strays. There were little bowls and dishes, and opened tins. When Catriona walked down the street, past the rows of doorbells and empty milk bottles, there was even the occasional saucer left on a top step, the surface of the milk crusty with dust. There was also the man who put out meat. She had seen him in the back lane; he looked about sixty, wore a suit, and he came out of the green back gate, the one with peeling, scabby paint, the house that had sixteen doorbells at the front. She wouldn't have paid him much attention except that he held out a bowl and called for the cats in a strangely high, thin voice. The cats clearly recognised the call: furry heads lifted and turned, backs were arched and stretched, and cats of all colours leapt off resting places, slunk around corners, and bounded towards the bowl. The man's feet were lost in a multicoloured snarl of fur, and within seconds the bowl was empty. A few of the lucky ones ran off to sit and crunch at bones, little delicate bones that splintered like chicken. Catriona hoped they'd choke.

One lunchtime in early spring when Catriona escaped from her office to sit in the unexpected sunshine in the park. The trees were still bare, but blue and white crocuses carpeted the lawns. She chose a bench in the sun, and sat with eyes closed, head tilted towards the imagined heat. But soon a shudder indicated that someone had joined her on the bench. She opened her eyes slightly and saw a man, trying to suppress her annoyance that she could not sit alone. But he seemed familiar, and she peeped again. She was almost sure it was the cat-man from the lane, but he wore an unfamiliar tweed jacket and cap, and was a little older than she had thought.

It was annoying, the way he fidgeted and muttered, and she was just making up her mind to move when he said: "Excuse me...I wonder if you could help me. What is the name of the spice that one obtains from crocuses? Or croci, I wonder if one should say?"

"Oh! I'm sorry... I don't –"

"You see, I've forgotten – wretched memory!" His voice was gentle, self-deprecating. "It's from the stamens – you know, the yellow rods, inside."

"Yes, I know which are the stamens." Catriona was offended. "Saffron."

"Ah yes. Saffron."

Illustration by Tash MacLeod

"Why? Are you thinking of collecting some?" She was prepared to be judgemental.

"Oh no! I merely needed that word. Thank you."

The man turned to watch the squirrel that had been stopping and starting among the flowers. His lips were moving, and sometimes his hands twitched impatiently. The squirrel reared on its hindlegs, then dropped down and scuttled towards a tree. The man gave a pleased little snort.

"Did you see?" he asked. *"That's* what I find so hard to capture. The skeleton itself must flow, and loop and turn." He was trying to explain with freckled, bony hands, as well as with words. "But the *words* must flesh it out, – almost disguise the structure. That's what I can't get right."

Catriona was embarrassed; she was prepared to dismiss him, possibly as a victim of some sort of dementia. Yet he seemed harmless, and one didn't often meet *interesting* people in the park.

"You don't see what I'm getting at, do you? Listen!

> Sinuous snake-shape slithering
> through saffron –

– you see there, that's why I needed you help –

> through saffron.
> That suddenly curls,
> furry fluffball,
> grey among blue and yellow goblets,
> uncoiling and *stretching*
> its bristling, prickling
> whiskered tail...

I haven't got any further, yet."

"Yes. I do see. I think." Catriona wasn't sure whether to be impressed, or wary of the old man's pretensions. "Have you done poems for other animals?" She tried to think of a suitable example. "How about a cheetah? Or an ordinary cat? You're fond of cats aren't you?" Catriona was sure it was the same man; but his face closed and his expression was blank.

"Fond of cats? No, no, I'm not *fond* of cats. There is no fondness in them, they do not reciprocate – they can only *take*. Good heavens, look at the time!" (He didn't even consult his watch.) "I must be going. Goodbye!" And he was gone, moving surprisingly briskly through the lunchtime strollers.

It was a few weeks before Catriona saw him again. She hid behind the damply-hanging towels and watched as he called the cats. This time he held the bowl high, out of reach, and pushed the cats aside with his foot so that one, and only one, could receive his gift. He walked backwards, encouraging the brown Burmese to follow, enticing it in through the garden door. The graceful animal stepped daintily out of sight.

He didn't notice Catriona that time, but saw her, a few days later, when the scarred grey cat leapt over the railings. Catriona had flung open the door and chased the cat down the lawn. The animal bundled itself together, unfolded like a flying fox and hurled itself at the far wall. It scrabbled and bunched its body against the stone, then pulled itself up, to sit, panting and glàring at its pursuer. She burst out laughing at its anger and then realised the cat-man was below her in the lane. He held a plastic bin-bag that hung heavily as the wind rattled rubbish on the stones.

"No, I'm *not* fond of them," he said, "and nor, it seems, are you!"

"It was – defaecating – on my lawn."

The elderly man continued staring up at her, wordlessly, until she became uncomfortable. "Mmmm...a lion rampant, gold on green."

"It looked more like a suction pad, with claws," Catriona said, puzzled, but trying to be helpful.

He looked at the angry cat, and smiled. "Yes. Oh yes. That's a nice idea. Thank you so much."

Catriona smiled back, and then went inside.

She poked the black bag with her foot, but it was ungiving and hard. She patted it cautiously with her hand, and its contents were curved and tall; since the bag was not heavy, she took it, and the letter, downstairs to her flat. She read again the poem. She cut the string and rolled back the neck of the bag: and stared into the unblinking glass eyes of the ginger tom. His broad face glared at her, his back was arched, his hair bristled stiffly round his neck, every part of his body signalling "Keep off!" Catriona stroked him; so cold and dead, yet skilfully reincarnated to such heat and fury. His legs, fixed firmly to the stand, were stiff and straight. She expected him to raise his tail and spray the cupboards, marking the kitchen as his territory. The ginger tom, captured, then recaptured in rampant gold perfection. As she, too, had been immortalised, and petrified, azure-tipped.

It was not until the weekend that she felt confident enough to respond. The poem had been unsigned, there had been no address, but the gift had laid a burden of uncertainty upon her that must be cleared. In her handbag she carried a small replica of a fossil fish, that she had purchased at the Museum gift shop, and had wrapped in blue metallic foil. The bones of the fish, compressed and preserved by aeons of hardening sediment, were starkly drawn as though by an engineer's pen.

Catriona's feet crunched on the poet's basement step and, thoughtfully, she pushed aside the small, crushed shoulderblade with her shoe. She rang the bell, but there was no answer, and the curtains were closed. A girl, going up the front steps, saw her and told her that he had gone.

"Three days ago. He's flitted – he was way behind with the rent."

"Do you know where?"

"No, he didn't tell anyone, just skipped. I hope he's got somewhere to go, though, he left loads of stuff behind. He must've been a bit weird, though – do you know what they found in there?"

"No." But she could guess.

"Cats! The place was full of dead cats, all stuffed and mounted. Really gruesome!"

Catriona shook her head in amazement, laughing with the girl, and walked away. She wondered if there had been a stuffed squirrel, too.

Dougie McKenzie

Shughy

Ma Shughy is a barry gadge,
No shy, no shan, a total radge.
When we walk oot they're aa impressed.
He only nashes wi the best.

Wi Shughy life is niver borin,
Saturdays his day fer chorin,
Make up, computer games an rings,
He ayeways chores me barry things.

He's only battered me the twice,
An efterwards wis awfu nice.
Broo the days the worst, eight pints o lager
An Shughy's lookin fer a pagger.

His chavvy is a radge cried Prince,
Half bam, half dug wi paws like mince,
If they stey in the hoose they're champin,
Their only luve in life is lampin.

Nae job, nae money in oor pocket,
The hoose is damp the stair is maukit.
There's hoors an junkies in the stair,
Wi Shughy here ah dinnae care.

Ah ken he luves me in his fashion,
Though half the lampins really nashin,
Ma ma says he'd be better single,
Ma Shughy he's a mental dingle.

Remembering Singapore, 1941

Auld yin yer tears are saut an warm
Ah feel yer hert beat next tae mine,
Yer greetin fer yer lang deid man,
Warm clay in Burma lang since syne.

Yer body's frush an bauchled bane
An yet yer dool is hale an strang
Ye luve me as yer very ain,
Yer loss has made us thick an thrang.

Did Christ hae sic a birn tae bear,
Tae thole sic sufferin sae lang.
Till trauchled roond an banged fu sair,
His saut tears sang the warld's auld sang.

It's aa by noo fer yince an aye
An Changis gates are lang syne steeked.
Yer but aa wumman at the bye
An roond yer pyne oor sperits beeked.

Pub Sang

Beyond the gantry sits ma luve,
Sae bonnie an sae braw.
Brichteened she soars the lift above,
The leam that lichts the daw.

The nappie flows, the bantry flies,
The reek an dirdum swal.
An where her nakit shouders rise,
The pintle jines the sawl.

She hauds the gless an slawly sips,
Warm flows the bluid red wine.
Fain wad ah pree frae these sweet lips
And tak her tongue in mine.

A haund she ligs upon her breist,
The preen upon her sark she frees.
Seily the mou whae gusts that feast
An feels her nipples heeze.

Her legs are souple, brent an lang,
Wi perted thighs that tice the leem.
Oft hae ah sowped the bree that sprang,
Frae that sweet, spicy stream.

Lang hae ah kittled as she thrust,
An skirled intae ma mooth.
Her sap a bumper tae the lust,
That slocks the lover's drouth.

Sune frae this fousome howff we'll flee
Scaulded, gyte, at last alane.
Then smool wi sleekit whispers slee,
Tae braithless mingle sawl an bane.

There wull we swacken limb, an loup
Wi merry skelp, we'll no be blate.
Wi dunt o hert an thrust o dowp
We'll tak life's canty gate.

But noo across this reeky haa,
Ah heeze ma gless an mak this hicht.
Far frae this fizz an fyke we twa,
Wull tent luve's bleezin licht.

Nicht Thochts

If ah could thraw the cauld wind's blast
An thole the end that's wrocht fer thee,
Nae glent tae backwards wad ah cast
Though ken ah weel it canna be.

We twa are cast upon this warld,
Thirled tae the yock frae oor tae oor,
Oor past is kent, oor vaig is harled,
An we maun live but tae endure.

Hush noo ma bairn the nicht is here,
The licht o day is smoored an deid.
Here in the dark my luve shines clear,
An fer this blink thy sperit's freed.

So sleep ma bairn nae harm or pyne,
Can mar yer slumber on this nicht.
The luve that bore ye lang since syne
Shines roond ye like a gowden licht.

An fer this nicht yer happit doon
Yer face is brent ma bonnie lass.
Smile in yer sleep ma bairn, too soon
Ye'll ken weel whit must come tae pass.

Faither

Faither, speakin as the child,
That hated ye fer runnin wild,
The man admires ye, aa yer rage
Wis sufferin dirlin at 'is cage.

An aa yer rantin, feckless drinkin,
Wis jist yer oot lood wey o thinkin
An breengin roond frae dram tae drouth,
Yer wee bit dialogue wi truth.

The red bluid on yer snaw white hair,
Anither fecht, anither stair,
Anither nicht o broken plates,
Wis jist yer discourse on the fates.

Fer men like you are gecked an dung
By thame wi words an siller tongue.
The only thing ye haes yer pain,
An Friday nichts tae keep ye sane.

Andrew R C Hamilton

Lust hits the diegesis dust

I trust, with all my heart,
you suffer not such conditions
as would render you farouchely,
nor that you are visited with
pre-menstrual, post-pastural or even
mid-lactorial invasions:
that, instead, you remain, as is your disposition,
baroque and sempiternal effulgent.

If, perchance, your downcast state arose
from thinking of me as an orchidectomised male,
let me confide in you what shall be
our crepuscular secret, my cuddly inamorata,
I admit to being somewhat steatopygamous,
with tendency to tumescence of the tum.

Listen, auscularily, to my heart
to hear the blood throb, indicating
a searching for release with you.
Please indulge not in *les mots croises*,
excuse my duncical knavery,
my umbrageous behaviour,
and be prepared to utter, on my behalf,
an innocent little fibette,
during this aestival season, and I shall not
make free with thy narrow loins.

Spelling Bee

"Children have to learn to spell well. It's most important for their after life." (John MacGregor, Minister of Education, on BBC2, 25.10.90)

If you can spell at age eleven
the Lord will take you into heaven.
But if you die and cannot spell;
I'm sorry, you can go to hell.

Another Nonsense Rhyme

Wee Willie Winkie
sat upon his pinkie,
thinking,
did Thinking Willie Winkie.

Along came a spidim
and sat down beside him,
growling and scowling
at Thinking Willie Winkie

I'll eat up your pie,
poke a hole in your eye,
unless you give me that pie
with the great big fly
you plucked from my web
and I'll bite off your neb
before I retire to my bed.

Should Willie comply
and give up the fly
or tramp on the spidim
that sat down beside him?

P.S. This nonsense was written when listening to Rachmaninov's Piano Concerto No 2 in the Children's Library in Kirkintilloch. It is strange what music and location can do to one when they work in unison, or, should I say, attack one's senses in unison.

It may be noted that a spidim is an insect like a spider but with an extra leg. This leg is useless and greatly annoys the spidim, making it particularly bad tempered.

Killer

John Saul

I, Donald Thomauske, thirteen years of age, being of sound mind and body, with glasses it's true, have decided. I intend, when grown up, to be a killer. Literally, of men: though I shall gun down my victims like dogs. The only reason I am not active already, now, cutting down respected criminals like Sheringham, or his henchman Bradshaw, is my lack of the necessary knowledge. I need familiarity with the usual security arrangements; the trickier ruses used to guard dangerous people. Also, *à mon âge*, I could not easily get hold of the right firearms. So you will find lemonade and my trigonometry homework in my school satchel, much as expected. The bulge in my anorak is an apple, not a grenade. Yet the day will come when I shall have a pistol in my briefcase. Not that I shall take it out in public, here for example, rise from my chair and coolly shoot Sheringham through the chest, *thunk!* No, I shall track him down patiently until five years from now he will take a holiday alone on the Riviera, and I shall gun him down in a backstreet as he saunters back, happy, drunk, to his swank hotel, *thunk thunk*.

So here I am: my school thinks I'm at a chess tournament, not an inquiry into licensing a disposal site for nuclear waste. I was at the chess, board 17, Thomauske, but conveniently dropped out in the preliminary round. I asked leave to stay on as an observer, but actually here I am at the hearing. Incognito but my dad knows. It will be chess in a more rudimentary form, he said. My mother shrugged. Anyway, here I can get on with bits of schoolwork should things turn dull. I can spread out: I've a whole suite of tables to myself. Sheringham, Transnuclear Fuels Inc., as he calls himself whenever it's his turn to speak, also has a suite of tables, to my front and right. But he has six advisers at the other seats, three at each side, all in a line. We sit in a vast prefab hall made of canvas and plastic and acres and acres of wood floorboard that makes the place sound like people were treading on gymnasium springboards the whole time. It's nonetheless very white in here, white up the sides, transparent overhead; cool and airy. I like to look up at where the great black loudspeakers hang down over us all from the roof; there's a whole fandango of speakers and lights and cables and electric fans up there actually. Back on the ground, also worthy of my mention and not to say nearest, on the world's lowest podium and facing directly opposite me and my tables, is the licensing authority. In theory they will decide if Sheringham, Transnuclear Inc., shall have his hole in the ground in which to dump every imaginable kind of nuclear waste. They intend to say no to him, it says in the local paper; but in practice, the paper says too, Transnuclear Fuels Inc. will win, tomorrow if not today. The licensing authority are my favourite here. They are *sympatique* even if they're weird sometimes; the chairman looks like my elder brother Richie and gets cheery all of a sudden when things seem to be tipping against them. I wave at him now and then; he waves back less often, but often enough, with a sort of laugh. ~

It's all right to shoot Sheringham because he's the lowest form of creature there is. You can sort of smell this about him. Though he looks clean and neat. To confuse matters further his appearance, his beard, his height, put people in mind of revolutionaries. But I know all of this is sham though, because I hear how he's received by everyone else in the hall, and it would take me centuries just to list all the parties present, but either they're angry with him or they howl back with dramatically sarcastic laughter, or they try and shame him, show him up, like the farmers did during their turn yesterday. They came in ringing cowbells and wheeling a load of harvest products in a great barrow. We hope we can go on harvesting things people can eat once you've done your dirty work here, was the gist of their message. They came round with baskets of potatoes and apples. I don't remember when I tasted such a good apple. A woman walked up to Sheringham and presented him with a big cottage loaf. This was an *événement*, and cameras shot out. Wait, he said. No unauthorised photographs. Incidentally this made it the only time I heard him say anything that didn't begin Sheringham, Transnuclear Fuels Inc.: his signature tune. As a matter of fact there are no photographs of Sheringham, authorised or unauthorised, I heard Dr Forsyth say. With or without this loaf. Though he won't have put a crumb of it within miles of his lips either or my name's not Donald Thomauske.

As I was saying, you can smell this essence of Sheringham. So far he's been called a criminal, a murderer, the filth of the earth, and a lousy, lousy fucking blood-sucking scum. He doesn't seem to mind. Basically he is prepared to put a stony face to everything. To put thousands, millions of people in danger or to death, so said Dr Forsyth down the microphone to his face on the first day, for a fat salary and a house in the mountains. One woman stood up and told him if anything happened to her children may he never sleep soundly again, because she could not say what she would do in revenge. Only that won't be necessary. Why wait until then, I won't. I shall already have dealt with Sheringham five years from now, six at the outside.

Presently, being just thirteen, I pretend I belong to those here that just don't know what to do. The helpless helpless, gape or laugh, throw your hands up. My father's generation, if I can go by the comics, would have turned their trigonometry worksheets into paper darts and thrown them. I believe we have become more sophisticated since. I have written suggestions about the hole in the ground and xerox-copied them on the machine in the press office, that's an empty room beside the main entrance here. Then I distributed them, like flyers, to the people nearest me. They don't mind this, they smile back, there's a friendly atmosphere in this part of the hall. I can leave my biscuits and satchel for hours and they don't get touched. Dr Forsyth, who knows I'm supposed to be cruising about going gawp gawp brain-rack at chess boards but won't give me away, even offered to lend a hand if necessary with my simultaneous algebraic equations. It's a pity he's a Z minus at the life of the Saxons; and as for French I could always teach him I suppose. *C'est la vie.* Anyway, there is this solidarity. You could say, the radiation experts apart (to the left and back, behind the council lawyers), everyone in this hall outside of Sheringham's own team hates his guts. And maybe they hate his guts too. So I know I'm in the right. It's just a matter of the logistics. My whole *raison d'être* will be devoted to the art of not getting caught. I have to get away with it so I can move smoothly on to the next deed; the hitlist is long, it's very long.

It's the security forces that are going to pose the toughest puzzles. When the farmer stepped up with her bread seven security men, dressed like the advisers only their suits were darker, entered at a flash through a sidedoor, chairs and microphones in hand. Before you could have said isosceles hypoteneuse they were sat squarely at the row of the tables behind Sheri's front line. As I heard a few people gasp I cottoned on quickly. Their microphones were even numbered like the others are (a control panel channels the voices to the loudspeakers, and at first you don't know where to look to locate any new person speaking); only their mikes weren't attached to the system at all. So it would have taken a brave farmer to have shot Sheringham dead on the spot. She just gave him this loaf though, and he smiled at her nervously, after all he knew better than anyone it could just blow up in his face.

Once I left not only a sandwich half-eaten on the table but also my lifeguard wristwatch, and it was still there an hour and a half later. I'd gone to see what was going on outside. You have to start somewhere. Sheringham's bulletproof car was permanently tended by two goons (viz. security men). You couldn't crawl through the tent sides without being seen. There weren't a lot of guards but they had their radios and could see everywhere, like soldiers on battlements. You could creep up on them as they turned about, I suppose, but why bother when it must be easier to tail Sheringham to his house in the mountains and see which plane he takes for his holidays. I didn't tell Dr Forsyth I'd been reconnoitering, but at one point he also suggested I took a look round, he said it only takes a short walk outside the hall to appreciate what an awful lot of money there must be to be raked up in nuclear power.

If I can go back to the farmers, on the side of their great barrow they had a sign that said NOT YET RADIOACTIVE. A woman in a yellow dress had a fit over this, and this is another reason they have to have so many goons. Most people are good-natured enough to accept their own fate, death, if it's perpetrated more or less decently (so I heard it explained in the row behind). But every now and then someone is going to flip out under the strain, what with Sheringham saying no, no, no all day long, day in day out, because every time he gets a question he squashes it like a cockroach, or passes it down the line to Bradshaw or to the lawyer, I forget his name, and Bradshaw squashes it like a cockroach, splat. So just like that, out of nowhere it came, *Arrgh!, Aargh!,* the woman in yellow started screaming, scream scream, but she didn't turn on Transnuclear Fuels Inc., she was screaming at a farmer and demanded he correct this piece of card by adding a question mark. NOT YET RADIOACTIVE? was what it should say. As they try to instill in us when we have a go at drama, it was an unexpected situation but everyone reacted wondrously in character. Sheri was stone-faced, though even he must have allowed himself a crumb of pleasure to see the opposition split so nicely. The environmental groups were sympathetic and asked for an adjournment; the chairman sent someone across to hear the woman out, to get a clear picture of what she wanted; I wondered if they entered "woman screamed" in the minutes; and courageous members of the public tried getting her to calm down. She wouldn't calm down, at least not for half an hour. Without actually touching anyone or anything, she went on ripping away at the farmer. They didn't put a question mark on their sign, not even after that. Then finally she broke into tears and sat there the rest of the afternoon session saying nothing and just sitting there with this most terrible broken look.

All this, I might say, speaks for my vocation, mon métier. I had considered other options. For instance, while I seemed to be gazing up at the speakers and fans a lot I did listen to the environmental groups. They argue, *ils se discutent*, which no one else does much. Other than Dr Forsyth when he gets the opportunity. I thought I might do that, work out the arguments and apply them, when I grow up, but I won't. Not because a couple of their lot gave me frosty stares for drinking coke from a tin; that was OK. How can I explain this. They have a man who looks like a rock singer and talks about the waste that could just conceivably come from a military base at somewhere called Mar*coule*, he gets angry too but I say he's cool, too cool, Marcool, he can get as angry as he likes and the hole in the ground is still going to get filled. And Sheringham actually wolfs up being offended, because that's one of his ways of dodging the questions. Sheringham, Transnuclear Fuels Inc., I must ask the respected questioner what he hopes to achieve by referring to me in such terms when I am attempting to answer his inquiries to the best of my knowledge and abilities, etcetera. Sheringham, Transnuclear Fuels Inc., I thank the questioner for her question but would be grateful if she could elucidate what bearing this has on the plans before us. Sheringham, Transnuclear Fuels Inc., I believe Mr. Bradshaw has already given a complete answer to this question, but if the questioner would care to reformulate the question, or to put a supplementary question, I would be more than pleased to provide him with a reply to the best of my knowledge and ability.

No, one day, years from now, there he'll be again. Sheringham, having lived the good life, will leave St Mark's Piazza, his hair going a bit grey and distinguished, his dinner jacket shining blue-black and his scarf white and silky, and as he turns into an alleyway *Moi* I shall shoot him down.

Vladimir Orlov

Chopped-up prose on freedom

This sensitises me to the value
of what humanity calls freedom.
In this context, however,
the meaning of this somewhat
sublimated notion seems poetic
rather than factual,
so often blocked out
by its adamant adversaries.

The poetic meaning of freedom
is certainly dim and obscure
enough to be bypassed.
But a rush of some forgotten emotion
now flashes through my servile mind
of someone who failed to inherit
this badly-wanted freedom
and now strives for at least
its poetic form.

Yes, in poetry any appeal to evidence
is at best awkward, if tolerated at all.
Poetry indulges our romantic
sky-based inclinations
and carries us away from reality.
But we poets share much more
than our inbuilt wishful thinking,
our desire for the obscure,
for the impalpable, for the sublime –
so often far too sublime,
someone will whisper.
We share our striving for freedom
which is so difficult to come by
in real life.

Darkness

Darkness closes at midday
darkness creeps into the evening
and morning which is to come.
I feel as if my blood now flows
out of me, with petrified flesh
left behind. I try to pull together
but I can't stand up to the onslaught
of darkness, I have always been weak!
and now am lured into being weak!

Offenders which are darkness
and the overwhelming power
of its underground generators
will never hesitate to tell me
to buzz off, as if I am that tedious fly
which always buzzes around
but which must rather buzz off!
That is not a moment to rhapsodise
the poor fly's adverse fate,
it's rather a call for patience,
an appeal to keep at least a single fly alive
and keeping to annoy you – just to show
how sweet and welcome
the anticipated stillness is.

From Under The Marble Tomb

It was caused by nothing,
aimed at nothing
but people's outrage.

Outrage, discontent, unrest...
All these heirs
of oppression
now send their menacing directions
all around the country
now caught up in complex implications
of its discarded past.

The unwelcome present
now breaks in on the petrifications
of what was sanctified
by multitudes of marching
purple, red, bloodstained, bleeding
banners now carried high
by the staunch pensioners
from our glorious past.

Their lofty calls
seem to chime in so well
with somewhat less lofty
cries of those "worked on"
in Stalin's prison cells,
now wafted to the marchers' ears
from the cells
of their tenacious memories...
The marching pensioners
crave for Stalin, whose death
let them out of the prison cells

but buried them
in those of their souls...
Are these people just the guns
he triggers off
from under the marble tomb?
The marchers never question.
They are called up from the past
and are here to obey.

The Dead Truck On Russian Fields

We waited for carts
near the local prison
where "enemies of the people"
were kept, their souls and bodies
envying the fate of the dead calves,
at least killed at once, rather than
after hours, days, weeks, years of torture
and everlasting abuse, death appearing
a tempting morsel, a gift of heaven
where Stalin claimed to reign.
Every morning and every evening
these dead calves sadly still alive
were been driven to Siberia's snow-hazed fields,
to camps to manufacture chains which
served to pull together the monolithic Empire
of Dead Calves.

Nobody grouped downwind of the calves,
as nobody could afford to be a human being,
not a calf, ready to be driven from
one department of the great butchery
of the Evil Empire to another –
sometimes a thousand miles away,
sometimes in your neighbour's room,
who informed on you to the secret police,
for you to wonder what made him do that,
but a hope to get your room for himself –
as award for allegiance.

And the "unadmired dropouts" were admired,
by millions of living dead calves around them –
shepherds were always esteemed, even though
everyone yearned to see them among the calves' herd,
welcome them in, brutally beaten and pushed aside
by new generations of shepherds and butchers
all ready to add up to the long butcher's list
as the pendulum swings yet again.

Shanta Acharya

In the Jagannath Temple

Under the *shamiana* of a tree
in the twilight of Puri's temple
sits a leper in the lotus pose;
Jagannath centred in his self.

His features reflected in the light
from the passing lamps of pilgrims
disturb the ambience of prayers
to the accompaniment of the temple bells
and the priest blowing the conch shell.

Grotesque anonymity fascinates;
the imagination similarly crippled
and irreversibly maimed
awaits the toss of a coined idea

To sustain its existence, *Hare Rama, Hare Krishna.*
Mouth holes frothing praises to his maker.
Gods emerge out of decrepitude when man
makes god in his image like some cruel joker.

The Poster Sticker

In the narrow lanes of Cuttack city
poverty secures for itself an eminence.

The wayside urchin hauls up a huge
colourful poster of Bombay's film stars
who return to him in his dreams each night
offering various modes of escape
from the drudgery of his daily life.

He is rich and famous like Amitav Bacchan
or young and dashing like Mithun.
Beautiful girls chase him; money is no constraint.
He is the local hero by popular consent.

His dreams are so real, he can feel them
like the silvery coins that are the sole reward
of his endless labours, day after day.

Short-changed, his Hema Malini slips
through the cracked sheets of the posters
that mock his lack of opportunity in such matters.

Desperately holding on to his dreams
as some talisman against the evil eye of reality,
he returns everyday to hoist his nightmare
newly printed on the pissed walls of this city.

The Unspoken

Once again resistant
flaming white icebergs

Out of the ocean emerge
in endless imbroglio.

The sunlight no longer
shines on anything immaculate.

I straighten the tippler in me
that stumbles leaning across

The dark cellars of being
and will not stay still

But watch for the moment alone
to torpedo these icebergs of silence.

Meditation in a bathtub

Condensation on the mirror
wipes me out of my orbit.

The rising steam of illusions
mould on the attic's ceiling.

Reflections blur
the world escalated
with thoughts' unredeemable patterns.

I, lady narcissus,
seek only the unperturbed surface,
a clean, white, deadly mirror.

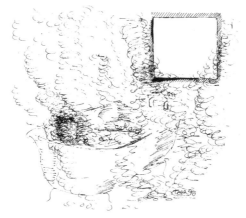

Illustration by Tash MacLeod

Manfred Malzahn

Consecutivity

Near in the distance lies Saturday
the twelfth – a date with the fragrance
of rosebuds (which may or may not be
for mothers) and mornings. At dawn
I draw in foolscap air
while wind walks barefoot on cobbles

Neither you nor I would have dared
to go anywhere near a May flower
and we might not have travelled at all
if there had not been some kind of April
(though I loathe Thomas Stearns Eliot
you are also allergic to cats)

Near in the distance lies Saturday
Mondays are for changing the past

Transfiguration

Is there a beast more peaceful than the cat?
Lavishly poured upon the sunlit sill
Of a silk-curtained window
She lies still
Enjoying all the comforts of the home
Content to be a languid rug of fur
And to adorn those places
Meant for her

But when the fluttered shadow of small wings
Taps gently on the pane, and makes her rise
We see her for a while with
Different eyes

Roused and tormented by the prey outside
Which mocks her in the splendour of her cage
She'd go and rip the curtains
In her rage
Were she not so well-bred and so refined
And thus she fends off all domestic strife
To carry on her dream of
Blood and life

The Busy Bard

Whan the new year blaws cauld and raw
The north wind dichts the hoose wi snaw
And maks us wish we were awa
Tae warmer climes
We may aye rise abune the thraw
Wi' fiery rimes

Rab, man, twas weel ye chose the day
Three dreich lang weeks past Hogmanay
We're ready fur anither fray
O' song and sonet
Ye sang the praise o hodden-gray
Sae leese us on it

But ye maun faik oor pretty air
Whilst we extol the hamespun wear
Designer wrappers, shouthers bare
On dally-dolls:
Ye nivver saw a dress sae fair
Nor teeth sae fause

Accoontant loons and banker billies
Clad fur the kill like Hieland gillies
They glower at the sonsie fillies
Juist woman-big
Whan they hear speak o Holy Willies
They're fain tae ligg

I wad ye're blithe at whit ye see
Forbye, the uisgebeathe is free
And the Immortal Memory
Will gar ye greet
I ken ye couldnae buskit be
Fur siccan wit

But whit's this, Rab? Ye will depart?
Weel noo, yon's swippert – tho it's hard
Tae shaw a wee bit o yer art
At ilka supper
Ye are juist wi us fur the start
And then ye scupper

Edison's *Tractatus*

Alasdair Gray

Perhaps you know that musclemen – hard men who want to be extra strong – have a habit of eating big feeds of steak and chips, and the minute the last mouthful is swallowed they heave big weights, or run great distances, or work machines that let them do both at once. This converts the food in their guts into muscle without an ounce of additional fat. When a dedicated muscleman overeats, sheer strength is the only outcome.

There was once a man who trained that way to increase his brain power. Not only after but *during* big feeds he would read deep books – trigonometry, accountancy, divinity, that class of subject – and concentrate on them fiercely and continually till he felt hungry again. He grew so wise that before you said a word to him he guessed the sort of thing you meant to say and quoted Jesus or Euclid or Shakespeare who had said it better. This destroyed his social life but he didn't care at first.

One day he was sitting in a restaurant reading Edison's *Tractatus* and beasting into his third plate of steak and chips when he noticed a young woman across the table from him eating the same stuff. She had cut it into small bits and was forking them steadily into her mouth with one hand while writing just as steadily with the other. She wrote in red ink on a block of the squared paper scientists use for charts and diagrams, but she was writing words as clear as print, so neat and regular that he could not stop staring at them although they were illegible from where he sat, being upside down. He noticed that the woman, though not a small woman, was neat and regular in a way that suggested a school mistress. He could not imagine what she would say if she spoke to him and the strangeness of this put him in a confusion through which at last he heard his voice ask if she would please pass the salt cellar, which was as close to him as to her.

The woman glanced at the salt cellar – at him – smiled – put her fork down and said, "What will I most dislike about you if I let that request lead to intimate friendship?"

He hesitated then said frankly, "My breadth of knowledge. I talk better about more things than anyone else. Nobody likes me for it."

She nodded. "What do you know about the interface between pre-Colombian Aztec pottery, Chinese obstetrics throughout the Ming dynasty and the redrawing of constituency boundaries in the Lothian Region?"

He said, "It's a perfect example of interdisciplinary cross-sterilisation. When William Blake said that *The dog starved at his master's gate predicts the ruin of the state* he was stating a political fact; the writer who traced a North American hurricane back to a butterfly stamping on a leaf in a tropical rain forest was reasoning scientifically; the absurd interface you posit is (like most post-modernist and post-constructionalist concepts) a sort of mental afterbirth. Are you writing about it?"

"No, but you can reach for the salt cellar yourself," she said and went on writing. The man felt a pang of unintelligent grief which he tried to quench with manly anger.

"Tell me just one thing!" he said sternly, "If we had conversed intimately what would I have disliked about you?"

"My depth of sympathy," she answered with a patient sigh, "No matter how loudmouthed, boastful and dismissive you grew I would realize you could never be different."

"O thank *God* you never passed me that salt cellar!" he cried.

And continued reading Edison's *Tractatus*, but no longer able to concentrate.

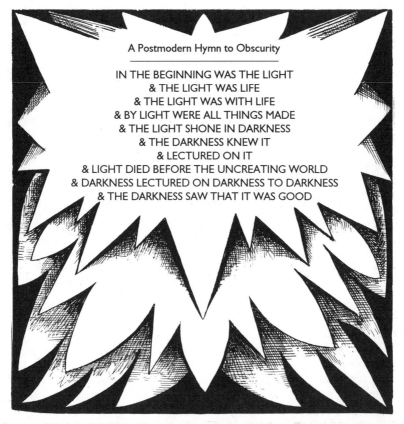

A Postmodern Hymn to Obscurity

IN THE BEGINNING WAS THE LIGHT
& THE LIGHT WAS LIFE
& THE LIGHT WAS WITH LIFE
& BY LIGHT WERE ALL THINGS MADE
& THE LIGHT SHONE IN DARKNESS
& THE DARKNESS KNEW IT
& LECTURED ON IT
& LIGHT DIED BEFORE THE UNCREATING WORLD
& DARKNESS LECTURED ON DARKNESS TO DARKNESS
& THE DARKNESS SAW THAT IT WAS GOOD

Ingredients Of The Foregoing Tale Chronologically Listed

1. In 1960 I went on holiday to Ireland with Andrew Sykes, a small stocky tough man with a thatch of white hair and a face like a boxer's who, like myself, never tried to dress very smartly. We had met when he was a mature student at Glasgow University and I a very callow one at the Art School. We were from the working class who had benefited when two postwar governments (Labour and Tory) decided that all who qualified for

professional educations might have them, whether or not their parents could pay. Andrew, who had been a sergeant with the British army in India, won a doctorate through a paper on trade unions in the building industry, getting his knowledge by the unacademic ploy of working as a navvy. This and a course in economics gave him insights into the working of our officer and financial class. He took malicious glee in gossiping to me about the insider trading by which this minority manipulated the rest. My notion of Britain had formed just after the Second World War when our government had been trying to make a fair society for everyone. I had thought Britain managed by folk who had mastered difficult processes through training and experience. Andrew explained that as much as any time in the past most civil service heads and business chiefs had stepped into senior positions because they had been to boarding schools and universities in the English east midlands: institutions where exams mattered less than friends they made there and their parents' wealth.

I thought Andrew disliked this system since he was gaining a good position by a democratic one. On our Irish holiday (guests of his friends Greta and David Hodgkins in Tipperary) I found he hated any group or party who wanted to change the existing system; the Campaign for Nuclear Disarmament, for example. He forgave me for being a member but we could not discuss it. I enjoyed what I saw of Ireland but enjoyed his company less than I had expected. He wanted self-government for Scotland but that seemed the only political hope we shared. His hobbies were wrestling and judo. He told me that body builders convert steak into muscle by a course of weight lifting immediately after a meal. Yet I feel, without being able to prove, that he and Ireland gave more to my tall little tale than the paragraph which starts it, so I will say more about him. He became Strathclyde University's first Professor of Sociology in 1967, retired in 1989, died in 1991. His closest relations were aunts who lived with him till they died long before he did. His job gave him prestige and colleagues; his holidays with Greta and David in Nenagh, Tipperary, gave him a family whose children regarded him as an uncle, a community which treated him as an equal. From a Labour Party member he became a xenophobic Tory. In the university staff club he once aimed a judo kick at a black visitor who was quietly minding his own business. His special study was trade unions and in the 1980s he was a salaried adviser of the British government, telling Margaret Thatcher how to weaken them. He took self-conscious glee in the bowler hat, tailor-made striped trousers, black jacket and waistcoat he wore on visits to Downing Street. I fear he did a lot of harm, but not to me. For fifteen years he was my only steady patron. He bought paintings, lent money when I was in need, usually took a drawing as repayment. He could lend as if it was unimportant, leaving my self-respect undamaged. He got secretaries to type my fiction, plays and poems onto wax stencils, for in those days photocopying was expensive, and printed all the copies I needed, without charge. In 1974 he arranged for the Collins Gallery of Strathclyde University to give the largest retrospective show my pictures ever had, getting a Glasgow Lord Provost to open it. (Sir William Gray: no relation of mine.)

Yet in his last fifteen years I saw him only twice or thrice, maybe because I no longer supported a family so had less need to borrow. After his retirement he became a recluse and a solitary drinker, his only human contact a cleaning lady and weekly phone calls from Greta Hodgkins in Ireland. I felt sad and slightly guilty when he died because he had given me more than I ever returned.

2. In the 60s I heard that Wittgenstein's *Tractatus* was a very brainy book. I thought it might not be too brainy for me but never got hold of a copy.

3. I am too shy and pessimistic to start conversations with strangers but when public transport and eating houses bring me near an attractive one I sometimes fantasise conversations. My pessimism ensures these never have happy outcomes, but one became the opening of play, later a novel, called *The Fall of Kelvin Walker*. In1982 I worked with three friends (Liz Lochhead, Jim Kelman, Tom Leonard) in writing a review called *The Pie of Damocles*. I scribbled out a sketch in which a young woman at a café table asks a depressed young man to pass her the sugar bowl and he insists on discussing what this might lead to before refusing to do so. My friends did not think this funny so I forgot it.

4. I started hearing the word *interface* in the 1980s. Folk used it to enforce the barrier which protected their work practice while talking across it. The barrier made the job they had mastered a safer source of income, but conversation across it might create new work, as forensic medicine had developed from the interface between policing and doctoring. My facetious attitude to new words led me into coupling activities between which no interface was possible. Around the same time I heard a lecturer amuse a university audience by referring to something as "an example of interdisciplinary cross-sterilization".

5. For several years I have been perplexed by the adjective *post-modern*, especially when applied to my own writing, but I have now decided it is an academic substitute for *contemporary* or *fashionable*. Its prefix honestly announces it as a specimen of intellectual afterbirth, a fact I only noticed when I reread my character saying so.

6. In some article a year or two ago I read that a scientist had shown how a butterfly stamping on a leaf in a tropical rain forest might precipitate a hurricane in North America. This may or may not be true.

7. In February 1994 I was going by train from Leuchars to Glasgow when I saw a young woman seat writing in red ink on a block of graph paper. I could not read her words but they were shaped with unusual clearness and regularity. She was bigger than average, neatly dressed and with no make-up or anything to catch the eye. I felt a strong prejudice in her favour, believing, perhaps foolishly, that she was unusually intelligent. I wanted to put her, exactly as she appeared, in a story. She exchanged words with a man sitting at her side but what they said did not interest me.

I broke my journey home at Markinch to visit Malcolm Hood in a nearby hospital. He and I were art students in Glasgow forty years ago and became close friends because we shared the same sense of humour. In 1992 he was paralysed by a cerebral stroke: his brain was in full working order but his body could give no sign of it. Today he can make signs and speak, though with difficulty. I feel guilty about how seldom I see him but unlike Andrew Sykes he has many friends and a loving wife. On this occasion, I read him a story from Somerville and Ross's *Experiences of an Irish R.M.* and snorts of laughter and comments showed his enjoyment. When students we often read out pages to each other from authors who made us laugh. My favourites were Max Beerbohm and Rabelais, Malcolm's were Dickens and Patrick Campbell. Campbell – an Anglo-Irish humorist not much read nowadays – probably gave us our first taste of Blarney, which I define as *the employment of an Irish idiom to make an unlikely story more convincing.* Somerville and Ross's tales are full of it.

Their genre resembles Conan Doyle's *Sherlock Holmes* and Neil Munro's *Para Handy* tales. They present a recurring cast of eccentrics in what now seems a small exotic world locked cosily into the era before the First World War. The magistrate's world is the Irish west coast at the start of the century. The Anglo-Irish narrator – educated at Oxford, Sandhurst and the British army in India – tells tales whose dramatic tension is between his own curt, ironical English and the speech of more native Irish who use words more inventively and ironically. The tales are garrulous with people talking to and about each other and enhancing the drama of speech to the detriment of facts, though the facts eventually emerge.

The new story was germinating when I got back on a homeward-bound train at Markinch. Most of it was scribbled in a notebook before I reached Glasgow and while I scribbled the words the voice I imagined saying them was an Irish voice deliberately constructing an improbable tale: that is why I eventually gave it an improbable title. Were I to read the story aloud I would do so in my own Lowland Scottish accent, but when writing "Edison's *Tractatus*" the sentences moved to a second-hand Irish lilt.

8. This lilt must come from a fortnight in Tipperary thirty-five years ago and renewed pleasure in Somerville and Ross's use of Blarney. Flann O'Brien's books are probably the greatest influence because, though Joyce, Synge and O'Casey use Blarney on occasions, O'Brien is the only Irish genius whose work is Blarney throughout. In the last six months I also enjoyed *This Fella I Knew*, a story by my friend Bernard MacLaverty who never talks Blarney nor writes it either, with the exception of this story. It is found in his recent anthology, *Walking the Dog*, published 1994.

9. When lecturing on creative writing in St Andrews University a student asked where I got ideas for stories. I gave a long, confused answer. Each novel, story or play seems to form differently. What set it going might be a story I had read which I wanted to tell differently, a daydream, or dream remembered on waking, or a fantasy I had evolved during a conversation, or an incident which had befallen someone else but was unforgettable

because of its oddity, humour or injustice. After that the idea grew through an alternation of deliberate daydreaming and hard writing. If the narrative expanded by drawing in memories, ideas, fragments of phrase which had lain in my brain with no obvious purpose, it became a novella or novel. All but my first novel came that way. (The first came from childhood faith in a long printed story as my surest way of getting attention, and happened years before I accumulated the ideas which formed it.) I have also developed stories by telling or reading them to friends before completion. Most authors avoid this because broadcasting unfinished work makes them less likely to finish it, but some listeners' suggestions have expanded my stories in ways which might never have occured to me.

The student's question made me hope you might like an account of what went into the last story. There must be more than I am conscious of, but I suspect the brainy hero is a caricature of both Andrew Sykes and me. We were both inclined to turn sexual urges into clever, sometimes boring monologues; but the urge to deliver an uninterrupted monologue is the energy driving every story and lecture ever uttered or written. "Edison's *Tractatus*" is obviously a portrait of someone too wordy for their own good, hence the addition of this bit of intellectual afterbirth.

William Oxley

History

(for David Perman)

I can see history wherever I turn
in the Letters of Hugh MacDiarmid or
the shell-lined grotto of John Scott
of Amwell, patiently, lovingly restored,
shored against blackboard oblivion
by a friend of the world and mine.
It is the unwinding silence in dead people's rooms,
a wind beneath churchyard trees,
the great world snake of perplexity
and the bloom of mind we call poetry.
It is chocolate-coloured snaps in time-foxed tomes
of those 'Way it Was' photographs
in souvenir issues of local papers
(that end up as chips-with-history!)
It is what sun scrawls on quartzy walls
and the challenge between tide and stone
that Sophocles lonelily 'heard on the Aegean';
it is the palimpsest left by everyone's dreams
whether of suburban Edens with privet hedges
or mythical Thules 'ringed with bright waters';
and I once saw it, history's river,
Amazon-green and soup-thick rolling between
purple cosmic mountains of sleep.
History, this more than nostalgia,
or seepage of past into present,
is the living dialectic of stones and man,
the long process of discovery of self-in-things
and the unlost memory of every loss
which like stardust falls on our tears.

Selecting the bushes

This one is small northern broom
that one mountain gorse
and here, winter-shrivelled,
is the so-like-lilac buddleia,
the House of Butterfly on Summer Street.
Where the spider has silver-planned
its web, and spittled dew drips,
and a 'cool-smoke' of mist

from Autumn's funnel
feathers down twigs,
I sweep away leaves
from tawny clawing roots
and out the mulch there springs
goblins, fairies, knights and norns –
a rash of mythic figures
(all from the rustle of a bush or two)
that gallop off through November air
to cloud-afforested shrines
and allegories of the mind.
And it occurs to me
someone chose these bushes,
Moses-like, because
they're full of burning tales,
or even only soggy stories.

Nostalgia

Why should we be moved
by long horizons, fish-backed seas,
our wires of feeling brilliantly earthed?

Laminated evenings over harbours,
tweedy figures straddling golfcourses,
lost chidren who were once our neighbours.

Why? Because, oh God, nothing
will ever stop coming back
through the sheer wild history of loving.

The mouth of poetry

I love to be awake in the middle of the night
And think of all the people that I know,
Hear the ticking of the small grey clock
On the mantlepiece where the gas-fire glows
And the wind that calls from out the sea
(That long white-silver plain beneath the moon)
And curls about the house then settles down in trees.
Love to think of other homes and other rooms
With their varied, different human smells;
Of the sadness sometimes or gladness there
And how, like me, so many of my friends
Can't help but seek the laughter and the truth
Of this ever dying, ever renewing world
In which to be alive in England still

Is more a marvel than a hell
Despite centuries of misfortune brought at birth
And the stupidities of every present.
For in the almost-silence of the night
Time's slow emptiness is full of thought;
And whether I summon John or Dannie,
Kathleen, Glyn or whom I will
Their own lives are very much a part of mine
Moving forever in the orchards of my brain,
Presences like angels stripped of plastic flesh
Who exist in memory or more than that:
In the unfinished tableau of perpetual light
Out of which we get our brief being here,
But which like the ingenious, playful wind
Or Walcott's sea-swift, or God, or words,
Is never finally anywhere, save in the mouth of poetry.

Oak and acorn
or the Lost Poem, not written down at its birth

On a village green an oak,
mountain among trees, that once had lain
like an idea of joy and pain
until, as at some silent word, it broke
from the green darkness of an acorn.

In this way all things get born,
but few more English-solid than this tree.
Evening was washing goldenly
over steeple, pub and common lawn
as doors of oak and all things opened up for me.

And I knew the point of being free
was to enter oak and acorn and wildly everything:
like the old man I saw gazing,
oblivious of me, simply at that radiant tree
and so into the all-inclusive heart,

the solidity of which we are a part.
Through acorns and swordy, lolling grass
the calm unstinted visions pass
as light-ringed swallows that dive and dart,
and one random hard-barked tree

becomes an epicentre of eternal beauty.
And one suit-crumpled gaffer the focus of
an inexplicable love: a love
that may well be the speechless divine
I recognise as his, if not as mine?

Crìsdean Whyte

Cumha Alasdair Chamshroin
2.III.1953–17.VI.1994

I

Bha siud cho luath. Cha mhòr nach eil mi creidsinn
gun tog mi 'm fòn uair eile na mo làimh
airson do ghuth 's e fonnmhor, blàth a chluinntinn

ag innse dhomh gach gobaireachd sano ilthigh
air neo biadh ùr a dheasaich thu, no leabhar
aosd' a bha thu air a cheannach. Thòisich

seachdainean do dheuchainn-sa air dòigh
cho àbhaisteach 's nach mothaich duine dhi,
le euslaint shuaraich a chum dhachaigh thu,

seòrsa cnatain bhig a thug buaidh air
do chluasan-sa. Is tu nad dhuine sultmhor,
bu bheag an t-iongnadh ged a dh'fhairtlich ort

thu fhèin a chumail dìreach ach le spàirn.
An latha a dh'fhan mi fad uarach ach cairteal
a' feitheamh riut sa chafaidh, 's a thuirt thu

gum b' fheudar dhut na rèileachan a ghlacadh
no bhitheadh tu air tuiteam, cha do thuig mi
brìgh fhìrinneach na cùise. Nach robh bràthair

do chèil' air caochladh mìos a-mhàin air ais?
Nach robh thu air do làn-chaitheamh, is tu
a' deasachadh a h-uile taic bho cheann

gu ceann an tinneis ud? Cha robh ach fois
is ciùin' a dhìth ort. Bha mi smaoineachadh
gum biodh tu slàn aig ceann seachdain no dhà.

Thòisich an laighe fhada aig an àm sin.
Dhachaigh air tùs, san t-seòmair mhòr, air uirigh,
gàrraidhean Athaill sìnte fodhad, tùr

an oilthigh dubh air fàire, eatorra
na craobhan beò le dòchas duillich ùir,
do theaghlach is do chàirdean mun cuairt ort

is tusa beagan frionasach, is tosdach
mar nach b' àbhaist dhutsa riamh. Cha robh sinn
a' measadh ceart truimead na cùise, ach

Christopher Whyte

Elegy for Alasdair Cameron
2.III.1953–17.VI.1994

I

It all happened so quickly. I can't believe
that I shan't once again lift the phone
and hear your warm, rich voice

giving me the tittle-tattle from the university,
or telling me of some dish you've prepared or of a collector's
book you've just purchased. Your weeks

of agony began so
unremarkably that no one noticed,
with a petty bug that kept you at home,

some minor cold which got the better
of your hearing. With your big mighty build
it is no surprise that you could only

hold yourself straight with the greatest of efforts.
The day that I lingered a full three-quarters of an hour
in the café, waiting for you, and you said

you had had to hold on to the railings
lest you fell, I failed to understand
the true significance of the situation. Hadn't your partner's

brother passed away only a month before?
Had you not exhausted yourself,
organising every aid needed during that illness

from its beginning to its end? All you required was
some quiet rest. You would be fine again
in a week or two, I thought.

Then began your long confinement.
At home initially, in the big room, on a couch,
Athole Gardens stretched out below you, the university

tower black against the sky, between them
the trees alive with the promise of fresh foliage,
your family and friends around you

but you somehow unsettled, silent
as never before. We were misjudging
the seriousness of the situation, but

bha 'n rùnaire san roinn fo chùram mòr
bhon latha a thàinig slugadh air do chainnt.
Cha robh thu fhathast air comas cainnt' a chall

ach thachair sin, san ospadal, 's dà chidhis
a' ceiltinn t' aogais, a' solarachadh dhut
an ocsaidein a bha dhìth air do sgamhan,

measgadh cho luachmhor 's gun do chuireadh tu
ach beag air mhisg, is siosarnaich mar nathair
a' sìor-thighinn asda. 'S ainneamh facal

a thubhairt thu bhon àm sin. Bha siud dìreach
do-ghiùlanta, nach robh dòigh ann air nochdadh
dè bha thu smaoineachadh, no faireachdainn,

meud do dhòchais, t' eu-dhòchais no t' fhiamh.
Thàinig sgàil air do lèirsinn mar a thig
cùirtean sìos ann an taigh-cluich', is cheil e

bhuainn gach strì, gach connspoid is gach strìochdadh
a ghabh àit' air t' àrd-ùrlar aonaranach.
Dh'fhalbh an niumòinia, ach dh'fhàg i

rudeigin na bu chealgaich na dèidh,
nach tèid a chlaoidheadh aig leigheas san t-saoghal.
Cha duirteadh ainm t' euslainte le neach,

ceithir litrichean 's nam measg a' chobhair,
mar gum b' e fealla-dhà bhorb a bh' ann,
an euslaint nach do chuireadh Gàidhlig oirre,

ach their mi rithe euceart, cruadal, olc.

II

Nad sheasamh bha thu
urramaichte, stàiteil, sultmhor,
ach na do laighe chuimhnich thu
dhuinn creutair cuirt' às eileamaid,
mar iasg trèigte air a' mhol
gun ghràs, gun chomas gluasaid.

Is dè their mi mud chèile gràdhaicht'?
Tha e mar neach a choisicheas
air lom na tràghad, 's àbhaist dhà
an t-uisge beò a bhith a' toinneamh
mu chasan, is an cop
na obair-ghrèis iomachaochlaich,
nach fhaic a-nis ach gainmheach odhar
gun dùil ann ri tilleadh mara.

the departmental secretary had had grave worries
from the day you started slurring your words.
You had not yet lost your power of speech

but that came also, in hospital, two masks
concealing your visage, feeding you
the oxygen needed by your lungs,

a brew so precious as to drive you almost
to intoxication, letting off a slow snakelike
hiss. You spoke

very little from then on. That was utterly
unbearable, that you should have no way of revealing
your thoughts or feelings,

the extent of your hope, of your despair or of your fear.
A film descended on your vision, as a
theatre curtain falls, and it hid

from us every struggle, every fight and every surrender
that played itself out on your solitary stage.
The pneumonia retreated, but left behind it

something more treacherous
that no cure in the world can crush.
No one spelt out the name of your disease,

four letters promising assistance
like some savage pun,
the disease which has not been put into Gaelic,

but which I will name injustice, hardship, evil.

II

When you stood you commanded
respect, you were dignified and portly,
but lying there you reminded
us of a creature driven from its habitat,
a fish washed up on the shingle,
bereft of grace, unable to move.

And how shall I speak of your beloved?
He is as a man walking along
an empty beach, accustomed to
the water winding playfully
around his feet and the metamorphic
lacework of foam,
who now sees only dreary brown sand
and no sign of the tide returning.

III

Bha dà ghalar ann.

Bha 'n ciad mar fhosgladh fòirneartach
gach dorais a bha nad chom
air dòigh 's nach b' urrainn dhut roghainn
cò thigeadh a-steach 's cò dh'fhanadh
an taobh a-muigh. Chan eil fhios agam
dè cho fad' 's a bha thu
san t-suidhicheadh ghàbhaidh so-leònte
gun dìon bho gach srainnsear mortach.

Ach cha b' e srainnsear idir
a bh' anns an dara galar
ach fear de na nàimhdean do-àireamh,
den phoball cheannairceach
a chòmhnaicheas anns gach aon dhinn
bho latha ar breith gu latha ar bàis,
a fhuair buaidh air do riaghaltas.

Chaidh do ghlacadh eadar dà shàmhchair
oir bha a shàmhchair fhèin
aig fear seach fear ded ghalaran,
sàmchair an nàmhad nad eanchainn
is sàmchair do dhì-armachaidh.

Tha mi claoidht' le sàmhchairean
oir rugadh sinn an dùthaich
nach eil gar n-iarraidh,
a bu chaomh leatha leigeil oirre
nach robh sinn ann idir,
ar beathan is gach faireachdainn
fhàgail ann an tosd
(tha mi gan cluinntinn a-cheana:
"Dàn mu Aids! Sa Ghàidhlig!").

Cò aig a tha fhios
nach eil an galar tosdach
a' dèanamh obair an fhuath aca fhèin?

IV

Is iomadh duine 'n Albainn,
an Lunnainn, ann an Ruisia,
taobh thall a' Chuain Shiar,
tha truagh an dèidh do bhàis –

III

There were two diseases.

The first was as if every door in your breast
had been wrenched open
so that you could no longer choose
who might enter and who would remain
outside. I do not know
how long you were
in that parlous, exposed condition,
defenceless before every murderous stranger.

The second illness, however,
was no stranger at all,
but one of the countless enemies,
from that rebellious population
which finds a home in each of us
from the day we are born to the day we die,
and it usurped the governance of your constitution.

You were trapped between two silences
for there was silence
in each of your illnesses,
silence of the enemy inside your brain
and the silence of your disarmament.

I am oppressed by silence
for we were born in a land
which does not want us,
which would like to pretend
we do not even exist
and kill with silence
our lives and our every emotion
(already I hear them:
'A poem about AIDS! In Gaelic!')

Who knows
but that the silent disease
is doing their work of hate for them?

IV

Many are those in Scotland,
in London, in Russia,
beyond the Western Ocean,
who mourn your passing –

Peadar do chèile dilis,
t' athar is do mhàthar,
do bhràthair is do phiuthar,
a dithis mhac 's a nighean bheag
a rugadh ochd miosan a-mhàin rod bhàs,
's i fhathast gun chomas èirigh air a casan.

Cha bhruidhinn i a-nis
ach san àm ri teachd,
aig ceann thall fichead bliadhna,
faighnichidh i:
Dè 'm fear a bh' ann an Alasdair?

Is freagraidh sinne:
Bu chridhe na fèileachd e,
làmh fhosgailte gun spìocaireachd,
aodann glan na bàidhealachd,
gun ghruaim, gun ghò, gun amharas,
beul cuimir snas-bhriathrach,
deas ri fealla-dhà is spòrs,
aigne gheur na tuigse domhainn,
an sgrìobhadair grad, drùidhteach, soilleir,
rianadair nan dealbh-cluiche,
an tidsear caidreach, brosnachail.

Bha gaol air aig gach neach a thachair ris.

V

Bheir sinn don a' chille thu
Diardaoin, an treasa latha air fhichead,
chan ann an sgìre t' àraich òig
no ann am baile t' oideachais,
baile t' obrach, t' ionad-còmhnaidh,
ach ann an Ile thorrach, rèidh,
tìr do dhithis sheanamhar.

Thèid do thìodhlacadh ri taobh
Loch Ghruinneart, anns a' Chille Naoimh,
fa chomhair na faire fosgailte,
's a' ghainmheach ga nochdadh leis
a' mhuir, 's ga còmhdachadh a-rithist
le ruithim sìothchail, ro-òrdaicht'
na iomlaid do bhualadh do chrìdh.

Air ciùine 'n àite, cha tu fhèin
an ciad ghaisgeach a chàirichear
mun rèilig aosd' a dh'iarraidh fois.
Is làrach bochd a-nis an eaglais

Peter your loyal spouse,
your father and your mother,
your brother and your sister,
her two sons and her daughter
born but eight months before your death
who cannot yet stand on her feet.

She cannot speak now
but some day in the future
in twenty years' time
she will ask:
What kind of man was Alasdair?

And we shall reply:
He was the heart of liberality,
the open hand that would not stint,
pure visage of kindness,
untouched by gloom, guilt or distrust,
the sweet mouth of polished speech
ever ready to jest and sport,
keen mind of the deep intellect
the concise, vivid, limpid writer,
the theatrical director,
the supportive, inspiring teacher.

He was loved by all who ever met him.

V

We shall carry you to your burial ground
on Thursday, the twenty-third day,
not in the parish of your upbringing
or in the town of your studies,
your town of employment, your place of residence,
but in flat, fertile Islay,
the land of both your grandmothers.

You will be buried by
Loch Gruinart, in the Holy Ground
facing the open horizon,
while the sand is laid bare by
the sea and washed over again
in peaceful, preordained cadence,
an exchange for the beat of your heart.

For all the calm of the place, you are not
the first hero to be transported
into the ancient cemetery to find peace.
The church is now a pitiful ruin

ach air latha blàr na tràighe
nuair a ghabh Clann Ghill-Eain an ruaig
shir iad tèarmann ann a broinn.

Chuireadh fadadh ris a' mhullach
is chaidh an losgadh, fear is fear,
neo-ar-thaing don altair choisrigte.
Cha bu lugha t' ionracas fhèin.
Theich Murchadh às is rinn e 'n snàmh
euchdach, claoidhteach gu ruig an sgeir
's dh'fhan e 'n siud fhad' 's a bha feum ann.

Air cho mòr 's a bha a ghaisge,
    cha robh do choibhneas-sa nas lugha,

air cho mòr 's a bha a ghàbhadh,
    cha robh do dheuchainn nas fhasa,

air cho làidir 's a bha ghàirdeanan,
    cha robh deas-chainnt do bheòil nas laig',

ge mòr a chùram air a shon fhèin,
    cha bu lugha d' chùram airson do chàirdean.

VI

Mairidh do chliù air sàilleabh sin
oir bhris mi 'n t-sàmchair le mo chainnt,
rinn mi luaidh air uaisle t' anam
's air fialaidheachd do chridhe fharsaing.

Le caochladh neul is drùidheadh shìon
is cagarsaich ghaoth sa Chille Naoimh
bidh d' chom a' dol na dhuslach glan
a shìolaicheas am measg nam fòd

is t' ìomhaigh nar cuimhne fhèin
a' fàs nas glain', nas soilleire,
mar sgàthan chaidh a dhorchnachadh
le anail eucorach do bhàis.

Bidh 'r dùthaich ag atharrachadh
's gach mac is nighean air am meas
le cothrom ceart, is t' uaigh a' dol
na h-àite naomh don fheadhainn òig.

    Chan eil ann ach an dòchas seo
    a mhaothaicheas mo phian a-nochd.

but on the day of the battle of the shore
when the MacLeans were routed
they sought refuge in its precinct.

A kindle was set to the roof
and they were burnt alive, one by one,
consecrated altar notwithstanding.
Your own integrity was no less.
Murdo escaped and by a heroic,
gruelling feat of swimming reached the skerry
where he remained for as long as was necessary.

Great as was his fearlessness,
*   your kindness was no less,*

great as was the peril he faced
*   what you endured was no easier,*

powerful as were his arms,
*   your eloquence was no weaker,*

though great his concern for himself,
*   your concern for your friends was no less.*

VI

Your name will live on on account of that,
for I have broken the silence with my speech.
I have spoken of the nobility of your soul
and the generosity of your big heart.

While clouds roll past and storms pour
and winds whisper in the Holy Ground,
your body will turn to finest dust
and filter through the banks of soil,

and the image of you in our memory
will grow purer and clearer,
like a mirror momentarily dimmed
by the grievous breath of your death.

Our country will change,
its every son and daughter judged
with justice and fairness, and your grave will become
a place of pilgrimage to the young.

*   I only have this hope*
*   to soothe my pain tonight.*

Translated by Michel Byrne

Photograph of Alasdair Cameron by Todd Severson

Mother's Pride – Jammy Side Down

Paula Fitzpatrick

Just before visiting, there was a mass exodus from the TV lounge. Eight or nine women in various stages of pregnancy and post-pregnancy got up and shuffled to the door. Someone told a joke. Three or four voices screeched approval. And then the room went quiet and I thought I was alone. Not that I really thought about it at all, slumped in a sagging couch, staring at a green-painted wall, lost in self-pity. When she spoke, it took me a second or two to pull myself together and before I could get focused on her she repeated the question, a note of irritation rising in her voice.

"Ah'm sayin, whit time do *you* make it?"

I glanced at my watch, absent-mindedly. "Nearly half-past."

"*Whit?* Whit did ye say?" she shouted.

She threw up an arm towards the wall clock. "Is that thing right, right enough? They –" (a nod towards the doorway) "they wis tellin me it's fast."

She leaned forward on her seat, staring at me with a look of outrage on her face as if she had caught me in a lie and intended to take matters further. It occurred to me that being pregnant is no guarantee of being sane – far from it. And she looked far from it to me at that moment. She also looked too young to have left school yet.

"Well, I make it just after twenty past", I admitted.

"Half-past's visitin. Ye said half-past."

But a lot of the tension seemed to have gone out of her as suddenly as it had come. She eased herself to her feet. There must have been only about eight stone of her, nearly a third of which was pregnancy. A striped, hospital dressing gown was belted over her bulging middle, a hem of pink nightie showed under the candlewick gown and legs like two white matchsticks ended in fluffy pink slippers. With her long, centre-parted dark hair hanging like rats' tails over her face, she was some sight.

She crossed the room and joined me companionably on the couch, sitting so close that the child in her womb could have kicked the child in mine. I shrank back a bit and watched her.

"Are ye havin visitors?" she asked.

"Not tonight."

My husband had only just deposited me at the hospital, driving in through an August downpour so heavy the windscreen wipers could hardly cope. I told her about it just to have something to say, described myself waddling like a duck across the car park in the rain, wondering how on earth I was supposed to follow Andrew's instructions and 'make a run for it' in my state. I had hoped to make her laugh but all I got was a pitying look and a knowing nod.

"Dumped you and buggered off home, has he?"

It wasn't quite how I would have put it but it was close enough. She took another look at me and grinned for the first time.

"Ye're certainly too bliddy late tae make a run fur it noo."

I patted my 'bump' and agreed.

"About nine and a half months too late, pet."

We both laughed, joylessly.

"See me?" she said, suddenly serious again. "See when Ah get oot o here? Ah'm aff! I never asked fur this, never wanted it."

I saw her searching my face for a reactionnt – outrage, admiration, anything – but I kept blank and silent not knowing what else to do.

"He's wantin tae marry me, Boyce is. That's his mother's idea. Next thing ye know Ah'll be knocked up again. Well, Ah'm no havin it. Ah'll make a run fur it okay, you wait an see. She kin huv the wean. Pair o heid-bangers, him an his ma! Got a fag?"

The only decoration on the walls around us was a huge poster warning of the dangers of nicotine. I tried not to let my gaze stray towards it as I shook my head. "Sorry, I don't smoke."

She tossed her hair back and narrowed her eyes in my direction.

"Ah'm gaspin fur wan."

"Sorry."

"Boyce is comin. He'll no bring me any fags though. Says it's bad fur the wean. Cheap bastard. Whit aboot me?"

She was on her feet again, restless and ungainly, shuffling around the room as if looking for some means of escape. I left her there. I got out when she wasn't looking, beat it to the safety of my bed and my magazine and hid from the other patients' visitors behind a copy of *My Weekly*, hoping no 'good Samaritan' would come across me.

Just as I was beginning to relax, I caught a movement out of the corner of my eye and she appeared, wandering the ward, her hair newly brushed and pigtailed over one shoulder, her eyes blank. She made straight for me.

"Ah'm supposed to be in bed. Visitin times ye're always supposed tae be in bed. If that old bat catches me Ah'll get jip. In bed durin visitin, that's the rules. Whit's the point though, eh? Whit's it matter?"

What could I say? I had an urge to tell her not to make trouble for herself, not in here, but I knew she wouldn't understand. If you asked her to look up 'trouble' in a dictionary, she'd have spelt it l-i-f-e.

She stood in silence for a few moments, looking across my bed and out of the window. Finally, she took the magazine from my hand and flipped absent-mindedly through the pages. "When are ye due?" she asked.

"Last week. I'm going to be induced tomorrow."

"Oh ay? That's good. Ah've bin here three weeks an they've no given me a date yet."

It began to look as if we might get a conversation going but our timing was wrong.

"Magrit!"

At the threshold of the four-bed bay, a man hovered shyly. Boyce, I supposed. Shaved head, black vest displaying tattooed arms, he was aged somewhere between seventeen and fifty-eight. All eyes fixed themselves on him. All eyes except hers. She stood with her back to him, not hearing.

"Magrit!!"

When she still did not respond, I politely drew her attention to her visitor and she turned and glared at him.

"Whit kept ye? Whit ur ye standin there fur?"

Her habit of firing questions seemed to have an even worse effect on him than it did on me. His face worked over as if he were trying to communicate with her through his eyeballs – sans use of mouth.

She stared him down, punishing him for his lateness and he was forced to speak, though nearly choking on self-consciousness.

"Whit dae ye keep wanderin aboot fur? Ye're never at yer bed!"

She ignored this and summoned him into the bay with a twitch of her head and they moved down to the chairs beside the window to conduct their visit while I retreated back behind my magazine.

They kept their voices low, her questions, his answers. The more she talked, the more he grunted and nodded. There was no doubt about who was laying down the law – much good might it do her! I had a sudden image in my mind of Andrew, an hour since, standing in the hospital corridor with my empty suitcase, nodding away while a hard-faced wee nurse gave him his orders, telling him when I'd be taken to the labour-suite and not to come in too early because nothing much would be happening for an hour or two. She didn't want him getting bored. As soon as she turned away, I got him by the throat (in a manner of speaking) and told him when I wanted him in. Never mind about being bored! And he went right on nodding and agreeing. I knew that when the morning came, he would show up whenever he thought best – no matter what anyone else said.

I tried to blot out their conversation, Margaret's and Boyce's, but it wasn't easy and I heard the 'end of visit' bell with relief. Before he left, Boyce reached into his jacket. Never mind flowers and chocolate, though, this man knew where his woman lived! He'd brought her a piece and jam wrapped in the wax paper from a Mother's Pride loaf. Margaret fell on the thing as if she hadn't seen food in a week. By the time I'd slipped out of bed, heading for a bath and the privacy of a locked door, she had strawberry jelly ear to ear and a look of childlike contentment on her face.

Our paths did not cross again for three days. An eternity in maternity.

It was well into the evening, visiting had just finished and I was on the hunt for fresh nappies in the store behind the nurses' desk. That was when I saw her. She was eating again. Someone had brought her a bag of oranges and she was sitting on the end of her bed surrounded by orange-peel. The air reeked of the fruit. She had no knife and her fingernails were bitten to the quick so how she was managing was a mystery to me but juice ran down her chin and neck and her hands were covered in a sticky mess. On the white bedspread, a yellow stain had spread around the discarded peel.

I didn't intend to stop, but my stitches slowed me down and she looked up. Our eyes met and I realised with a start that she wasn't pregnant any more. What could I do? I had to be polite. I smiled but she didn't smile back. I began to doubt if she even remembered me. The woman in the bed opposite was watching me curiously, making me feel uncomfortable. I thought of Boyce and wondered if he had been responsible for the oranges.

"You've had your baby then?"

I gestured towards the hospital crib beside the bed.

"Boy or girl?"

Without taking her eyes off me she lifted a chunk of orange to her mouth and began to work the flesh from the skin with her teeth. I shuffled across to the crib and leaned over, causing an immediate wail from the baby which made me recoil with embarrassment. I straightened up and smiled at Margaret apologetically but she let her gaze drop long enough to reach for another orange. Then, watching me closely again, she broke the peel with her teeth and began tearing the thing apart with her blunt fingertips.

The wail from the crib rose to a crescendo but neither of us moved. It was dark outside by now and the overhead lights were on in the ward. I became aware of my own reflection, pale in the glass of the window behind her and behind the shadowy me, the moving lights of cars on the distant motorway. I was going home in the morning.

"Ah well, feeding time again, eh?" I said.

She spoke at last then, but she spoke quietly without any of the former fire in her tone and her mouth was full of orange so it was hard to make out what she was saying. Only two words came across clearly:

"...bugger off..."

And so I left.

Ron Butlin

Advertisement

Would you like a very Scottish servant all your own
who'll do for – spiritually speaking – you alone?
A lad o' pairts – a prophet, historian and more,
a therapist/composer who understands the score?
Guaranteed – your past and future contrapuntally combined
into a pre-determined present so defined
you'll never need to think or feel again!

Your gardener for life, his motto: prune first then restrain
the slightest sign of growth. He'll cut you down to size
(for your own good) then train your roots to do
their darkest: dig deep, grasp, immobilize –
if needs be, split your soul in two.
He'll anticipate your every beck and call –
he kent your faither, after all!

As a Scottish-school economist he takes great pains
where pain's no longer due. He's no credit-giving Keynes
– he'll soon have Adam Smith's close-fistedness outclassed,
insisting every childhood trauma last
your lifetime. All you'll need to know is what he'll tell you
– even when you're sleeping he'll compel you
treat his dreams as if they were your own.

Say 'Yes' – he's yours! Your very own: flesh, blood and bone
passed on as Scottish fathers pass him on
to Scottish sons (with references supplied
unto the seventh generation). A tendency to patricide
but nothing serious – just words – so never heed him.
This very Scottish servant
– who needs him?

The Start of the Affair

We've torn the moon in half and kept the darker side.
Turn out the light.

Shadows of a man and woman touch and then let go
– these, the only truths they know,
are trapped between the only words they dare not say.

Turn out the light but do not turn away –
one fragment of the moon brings night.
Its ragged light is all we have to see by.

Histories Of Desire

That was when I threw the stone and then ran after;
splashing into Smallholme burn I made the colours
of a summer's day cascade around me.
That was when the water stilled to rowan-berries,
clouds and dark green leaves I could never reach
before. I tried to pick one up –
that was when the earth and sky first slipped
between my fingers.

All histories are histories of desire, they tell me
how my life begins and ends; a stretch of water,
a stone a child sends skimming
to the other side.

At Linton Kirk

Linton Kirk is stone and timber hollowed out of air
where stained glass darkening to a patch of shadow, traces out
a present tense across the floor.

Our first weekend together: a night without much sleep,
a morning's levitation over hills and cold rain.
The visitors book lies open. We flip the pages back
to catch sight of a world before we'd met,
then pause uncertain what to write. I glance outside:

an East wind scours the burnt yellow fields to black,
tearing colour from trees; the blunted edge of winter sunlight
hacks at names, dates and words of consolation;
the dead withdraw into the living.

Your scent, the colour of the scarf you wear,
our closeness – these are not memories.
Once we've signed the book and put the date we'll leave
and Linton Kirk stand empty.
How far into the future can I reach to take your hand?

Life-line

The old woman took my hand in hers to trace,
as best she could, the lines (some broken, some
complete) upon my skin – signs, she told me,
of the man I would become.

Quite suddenly I flinched at an imaginary pain:
– this wound was slashed across my open palm.

The Kiss

Penny Glenday

It had been a good party. At some point Miranda had the idea of painting his fingernails a vivid searing red. He hadn't been the only one – by the end, almost half the men there had succumbed... at least one had also red toenails, and another was begging to have his foreskin anointed too.

"But I am above that", responded Miranda haughtily, as she whisked from one group to another, cajoling, crooning, winkling out the fingers and capturing their owners' attention from the assault on their pinkies by pressing her breast against their arms, and looking deeply into their eyes. For most, it was a good deal, those few moments of unequivocal bliss... not quite worth the problem the next day with brillo pads, penknives, whatever, as they scraped the clinging shards of dried red from pink-stained fingers. Well, they could hardly go out for the *Sunday Post* with painted nails, could they? It would be the talk of the village.

But they weren't thinking of that while they held fingers still, they were just enjoying the brief intimacy, sanctified because it was under the very eye of wives and lovers even, who just smiled indulgently. They knew Miranda too well to worry; in fact it brought out a protective streak in them, seeing their tall and manly men reduced to simpering idiots by her.

If gossip and hints are to be believed, those red nails enlivened many a routine Saturday night encounter... the women softened by seeing their partners weakened as efficiently as had Delilah shorn their locks. The men, unaware of their wives' newly-reawakened tenderness, simply enjoyed watching their own hands, suddenly soft and female, slipping over pale skin, and they spent hours more, touching, gliding, maybe just fantasising a bit that it was Miranda there...

Miranda, who pressed small breasts against them, whose hand drifted so tantalisingly close to private parts, seemed oblivious to social convention as she kissed wives sedately on the cheeks, but greeted the men lips on lips, lips wettened by a tongue that barely flickered out, like a snake's, seeping through the grass. So the hours slipped by, glasses miraculously never emptied as Miranda flashed by, interrupting all serious political discussion, the earnest literary debate, the inevitable talk of toilet training...

"Blood?" she'd suggest, holding up a bottle, and then giggle when white wine gushed out. "I don't know why I do that", she'd cry, and be off again, same bottle, same question... and same surprise as the bubbles gushed out, pale as pee on a picnic.

"Listen," she'd say earnestly, "I'll get you red, I'm sorry, I really thought..." and the men would laugh, and say it was all right... but somehow she never got it wrong for a woman. Yet she wasn't a flibbertigibbet. She flirted, but she leaned against women too, her pupils dilated as she launched as happily into an attack on health visitors as prime ministers. Even the women didn't resent her intrusions... her prattle, her bright enthusiasm. She was a gossip, loved tittle-tattle, but who could be angry at her when she so happily prattled about people to themselves? She would skip back across to the latest source, demand to know more and slip a confiding arm around them as her eyes and mouth widened, a smile touching the lips, lighting those eyes. She was incorrigible, but as no one cared to change her, it didn't matter, did it?

But the kiss. It might have been only a kiss, but it was so unexpected. When Miranda had encouraged Jane, who was in the throes of a messy divorce, to paint her nails to match her own, and then to paint George's, her aim had been honestly to engineer an affair between the two. Tall and artistic Jane. Fat little George with the gentle eyes and soft little hands.

"Well, I could hardly say, here is a debonair widower, who has no real need to get too involved and here is a nearly-divorcee who looks as if she could do with a good screw, could I?" she had asked another friend, who knew both parties and could be relied on to repeat it to each. She'd been feeling rather generous of spirit, actually, but willing to swop her vague stirrings of jealousy for the titillation of watching the passion evolve.

Slight error of judgement there, she'd decided. George had looked at Jane with interest at first. Mid-forties, she was not pretty, but attractive enough with her generous mouth and gappy teeth, and he'd happily offered his podgy hand to have his nails painted, and dally a while thereafter. What he, or Miranda, hadn't expected was her reaction, which was cool. Miranda later realised that if she hadn't been so subtle, Jane (who indeed did want a screw) wouldn't have thought George was Alison's bidie-in. So George had slunk back to lean against Alison's chair. Alison, who'd known George a long time, absent-mindedly stroked his hair... confirming for Jane her misconception. While she stroked and George purred, Alison looked across at Alfred, who was indeed her bidie-in, and hoped that it would soon be time to go home because she had period pains.

Alison sighed as Miranda descended on Alf, kneeling at his feet like Bloody Mary Magdalene, her own red nails flashing as she painted a toe... Her tongue protruded just a tip as she concentrated on Alf's foot, beginning to smile at a joke he cracked, before effortlessly countering with one even filthier, even funnier. Alison had known Miranda a long time, and sometimes resented her easy manner with men. In fact, she thought (just a touch bitchily), Miranda's total success was simply because in spite of all the breasts being pressed and bums being touched, Miranda was a bloody prude and absolutely *everyone* knew she was no threat whatsoever.

George also watched Miranda, and Alf's slender feet, and when he considered his rejection earlier was not too sad. He didn't really want any complications and could rely on Miranda to complicate anything she had a hand in. He was having it off with a secretary at the office, anyway, and didn't feel too deprived. So he sat, admiring his fingers, and without realising it, became rather camp in his movements. His cravat seemed more dandified, his cardie suddenly quite the thing, and when Miranda flounced back in with more wine, he'd positively oozed the homosexual at her.

Needless to say, Miranda had loved it, and dragged him round, introducing him as their token ageing queen. Those who knew her knew that she was not in the least homophobic. There were at least four gay men there, and they smiled tolerantly at her, their fingers still as pale and carefully manicured as they'd been at their arrival.

But it worried others. She had earlier introduced a TV presenter as "our token famous person", and had berated the fact they didn't have a token black. Close acquaintances knew not to think twice, but one or two spouses, were a bit put out. "She's a teacher, she oughtn't to be like that! She can't mean it, surely not…" they'd clucked and cooed to themselves.

So Miranda, clinging to George who was becoming outrageously feminine, was freed from being flirtatious. George, who was genuinely enjoying the freedom to express the urges and sensations he'd repressed so carefully all his days was the perfect partner. Miranda softened, left her husband to pour the drinks, and lolled on the floor against George's round body as she sympathised with Alison about belly aches, and listened with, for her, devout attention to Alf's political ideology. Alf had spoken seriously, his eyes fixed on George's face, and George had nodded and smiled.

The night went on, people drifted away, and towards the end when everyone else was in the kitchen, not realising they were all that was left, George had quietly drawn Miranda into the empty sitting room, leaned back against the door and pulled her closer.

Just a kiss, a kiss between someone who played the nymph, but seldom was, and someone else who really didn't know why he was doing it, when he really wanted to be holding and kissing Alf. Maybe he recognised the maleness in her, in her small breasts, flat hips and cropped hair. Maybe she was misled by those soft fat little hands with the painted nails, but neither expected that kiss to burn as it did. Lips sought, touched, broke only to seek again, her body pressed in against him, his hand swept up against her hip, to her breast, cupping it, pressing it flatter, as she sank into him, drowned in him, as he sucked, nibbled, licked her neck, her throat, those lips, pale now the red lipstick had been left on countless cheeks and glasses of wine, white as pee. They heard voices and broke apart.

It was not for several minutes after that she was able to identify what had been odd. But press as she had, his round little tummy, as roundly pregnant as hers had twice been, had stopped her pelvis reaching down and round. "I don't even know if he, I don't know…" she'd thought, needing to know just how good it had been for him. Then she'd waved him goodbye, and Alf and Alison, and had filled the dishwasher, moving round the final guests who drank coffee and sank maudlin heads onto arms on the table. She brushed against one man as she passed, wanting the comfort of the predictable, and finding that she and he, and they, felt nothing.

The kiss, only a kiss. Nothing wrong in that, except that kiss had hurt her. It had left her belly melting, her genitals burning, her lips aching… and she didn't know how he'd felt.

Miranda knew she should leave it at that, but a week later the ache was still there. "I need to kiss him and feel it against me", she had muttered one day, in front of a class, who – used to her – didn't listen. But how on earth to achieve it? Her problem was not so much arranging a time or date, although that proved harder than she'd anticipated. The trouble wasn't even in her justifying her proposed infidelity. Well, sometimes you had to flow with the tide, you had to occasionally break the rules, didn't you?

She pretended to herself that all she wanted was to be kissed again, but kissed so that she could feel his excitement, and know that she could make him feel as helpless against the rising surge as she had been.

She thought about it as she peeled potatoes, bathed kids, marked jotters. And in fact her pupils smelt her indecision, and enjoying her mellowness, relaxed and sat back, watching her eyes sparkle and grow dim as the memory of the lust swept over her. She taught 'My Last Duchess', 'Come Let Us Kiss And Part', and the boys didn't even complain. They too caught the agitation, and sought out girls in the evenings to kiss and press against.

Miranda was not one to fail. Waiting until her husband had to go away for a night on business, she bedded the kids and phoned George. It took two hours of whispered pleading, heavy breathing and exchanged confidences to entice him over. She opened the front door before he rang the bell, led him, two glasses and a bottle of wine up to her bedroom, where she'd lit the fire, and primed the cassette. But it had been wrong somehow, a bit one-sided. Almost immediately, he rolled against her, kissing her briefly before moving down. She lay back, gasping and moaning more for the loss of her fidelity than anything else. So while her body writhed and jerked, douce and obedient to his tongue, she sat a bit apart hoping that she wouldn't have to reciprocate... What's the good of a one-handed clap anyway, she'd thought sourly, and realised that she had wanted to talk about the others, and laugh, and complain about colleagues at work who rigged the marks, and sod it, this might be efficient, but it wasn't fun.

George, feeling her body judder and deflate, foolishly thought he'd done what was required and felt it a fair deal. He'd learnt something the night of the painted nails, and decided that when you were forty-seven, you might as well indulge yourself. Alf had no intention of leaving Alison, but every intention of returning to George's flat... he'd been amazed when George first kissed him... but, well, you can't live by the book, can you?

George followed her down the stairs. He didn't notice that Miranda was grieving and reached out to her. Still standing on the first step, he was taller than her now, and as he kissed her... his chubby little hands slid round and pushed her bottom in against him.

A kiss, just a kiss. But it was tender, it was familiar now, and it warmed her grieving soul so that she cleaved against him, and wanted to tell him to stay, and let her make love to him. But he was thinking of Alf, and the little bottle of lacquer even now in his jacket pocket, and how he would paint his nails a rather fetching tangerine shade tomorrow night, and how those little plump fingers would look against Alf's white belly...

And later that night, lying alone in the big bed, Miranda had decided that she would never again let that happen. It was too dangerous, for George fancied her, and would probably get ridiculous ideas. It couldn't go on.

But she smiled as she remembered the kiss in the moonlit hall, his lips, his hands... and oh, that bump against her thigh.

Tom Pow

Lemons

Rilke's wager: ask yourself
in the quietest hour
of your night, Must I write?
Confess to yourself whether
you would have to die
if writing were denied you.

❖

He lay in the early
morning, blankets over
his head to muffle the cries
of his son. Through the small
window he could make out
the mistiness of day

the last apples rotting
on bare branches and these
against sky the colour
of dead fish. His head still
thick from the night before
buzzed with ancient guilts.

He felt he should concentrate
on blackness, stillness, a
kind of depth though he felt
hollow in himself. First
that question: ask it now,
his body sprawled alone

with its night odours. Yes,
he would still have the strength
to answer it, to hoist it
over his drowsy form
long enough for a green light.
He did and the answer

was no. No he didn't
(and wouldn't). He'd had to
once, but now he didn't.
As the question dissolved
energy surged through him.
He saw the day unfold.

He'd give himself
to his wife, to his son.
"What would you like to do
today?" he'd ask, now
he was free, free to do
whatever he wanted.

He saw a future fresh
with possibilities –
job options, new hobbies,
simple ones. He'd become
a Regular Joe. Sunlight
chased the mist, bathed the room.

He tried to remember
how he'd got into this.
And the others – the poor,
the proud, the abstracted –
let them get on with it.
He was open to the world

like it was a clean page.
And part of what he saw
was what she'd always said
he missed, brooding about
blaming the rich world for
the poverty of his own

imagination. And here
it all was, the detail
that made up this fresh
new world; the bowl of fruit
and vegetables that sat
on the table where each

morning he took coffee.
The onions' smooth tan skins,
the tight-sheated tomatoes;
the nipples of lemons
were loud in their own praises.
He smelled them all, rolled them

in his palms. Lemon groves
he'd walked down in his youth
came back to him, starlit
nights that never grew cold
that he'd shared to the sound
of the sea shushing in.

And the sea took him back
to "the royal richness"
of childhood, "the treasure
house of memories." But
this time he saw it crash
onto rocks, felt the salt

sting his soft cheeks. His wife
had told him of this world,
that it was all around him.
Why had he not listened?
Why had he not noticed
how beautiful her faith

in it was as it shone
in her eyes and lit up
her face? So love was there
to be discovered too
in this new unwritten
future. So much! So much!

And he'd proved himself right.
He wasn't dying, nor
did he think it likely.
Still, he thought, take no chances –
if you're going to go, be sure
to take those lemons with you.

O Canada

("Below 60" – Whitehouse, Yukon.)

In a redlit space the size
of a small parking lot, seeking refuge
from bright, educated Canadians,
I sit at a bar whose gantry consists
of a huge floodlit case of bottles
of beer and vodka mixers.

"Fuck you, white man!"
Harry calls me over to say,
beading me with brown eyes,
brows gathered beneath his baseball cap.
Then he wants to crush my hand in friendship
before punching an open palm –

"I'm a man but I'm a cat.
Watch it!" A solitary drinker
responds, "I'm a fuckin' Canadian."
Red, his full, wet mouth not quite
hidden by a grey spade beard, mumbles,
"I'm a survivor."

The juke-box is doused
for the outcome of the Referendum.
"Harry'll know the results," says Red,
"cause he's an FBI –
a fuckin' big Indian. Now go on Harry,
fuck off...He's one of the best,"
Red tells me, as Harry leaving hold
of our shoulders stumbles off
back to a group of natives pouring over
a globe of silence. "Yea, never done
a day's work in his life. Not that I know of."

"Canada's great OK!"
Harry shouts at me across the room.
"Greatest country in the world," Red nods.
"Why? Cause you can do
what you want. That's why."

"Fuck Quebec!" the solitary concludes,
encapsulating one view of the night.
He tosses down his short
and slips off his stool. "I don't give
a fuck!" This of course is the language
of compromise for which Canadians
are renowned over the whole
fucked-up world.

Outside in the crystal cold
I walk the frozen empty streets
feeling that largesse, that bonhomie
given to those who know they walk
the streets of the greatest country
in the world. Back to Hotel Taku –
Taku in the native language, a flight
of geese and a goose that's cooked that's me;
the only thing stopping me breaking into

O Flower of Scotland
When will we see your likes again?

that Whitehorse Star headline buzzing
in the back of my mind: "Coyotes
Are Hungry And Your Pet Will Do."

Pigeons

"There is something poisonous about the cultural climate of a country inhabited by creatures who pollute the environment by wasting the time and tolerance of other creatures unfortunately conditioned to take the crass creatures at their weary words."

Alan Bold on contemporary Scottish poets who give readings of their work. (*The Herald*, 3 Jan 94.)

Excellent poets in distant lands, the world
can't shrink enough for any of us! Sheer chance
brings me to your work – a raft riding

white waters doesn't care who it carries.
Oh I'm intoxicated now! though for years
you were beached on another's shelves, your art

a gentle forbearance as you waited
to begin your shy salaams. Yet you've so much
to say! Surely anyone can see that now –

though the ghostly audience you claim
is scattered amongst your own folk, the ones
who more or less ignore you: deny it

if it's not true. And I only say that
for we share the same self-deprecating
armour-plated jokes and a similar taste

in friends. Do yours read you either I wonder
or simply buy your books but love you
for quite other reasons? I wonder too

do your good critics use words like 'shameless',
'ponce' or 'poisonous' in their descriptions
of you? While I ponder this latest

sad flyte, a memory floats into my mind
of a reading I once gave with Ron Butlin
to a scattering of students in Moscow

before the Union finally fell apart.
The site was their professor's littered office
where mounds of paper spilled from desks, old maps

of the red world hung from flaking walls.
He himself was so urbane, the marble
in his mouth must have been bought, with compromise,

abroad. "What do you think of Muldoon?" he asked.
And Dunn? Larkin? he knew them all. Did any
of his students write? he half wanted to know

yet seemed more interested sifting
through those papers. (Let no one be in doubt
he was an important, cultured man – but oh

what he'd had to preach that he despised!)
A girl with long black hair, fine-boned in cheek
and jaw, raised her hand. She was from distant

Tajikistan and in her own language
read a poem with rhythmic, sensual soft
sea-sounds. It was translated into Russian

and then, for us, into a halting English.
When she came to Moscow she was lonely.
The leaves in autumn fell, brushing past her –

and here now, as she read and translations
were made, a buttery light filled the room
and quietly lay over the dusty stacks.

She remembers autumn in her home village,
and her family and friends and she hopes
to return there some day soon – to a land

steeped in blood, whose fruits are rich and various;
a land swept by countermanding emotions. Once
they were peaceful herdsmen there. Always

we have been conquered, she says. As we listen
we feel strongly the love in her poem, a gift
that enriches both our day and hers.

Ah but if only, the poem continues,
we could rule our hearts with the simplest
of commandments: drink only green tea, avoid

the unwashed and open fruits, then perhaps
we could all live beyond history; perhaps
we could clear the shadowy foothills

and arrive at a place where the peaks are sharp
and the prospects clear. Years later in autumn
again I think of love and translation,

watching pigeons with a restless energy
wheel and turn in a cold grey sky. Sometimes
the moment chimes and the effect is more

than rhetorical. But mostly there is only
solo flying and each of us rising through
the poems through which we must pass,

shaping the landscapes as we pass, rising,
rising till our raft of voices fractures
and we sink back into the buttery light.

Reviews

Time's Encomium

Beside The Ocean Of Time, George Mackay Brown, John Murray, £14.99; *Imelda*, John Herdman, Polygon, £7.95; *Red Tides*, Dilys Rose, Polygon, £8.99

Beside The Ocean Of Time by George Mackay Brown rates amongst the best novels I have read this year and is, to my mind, his greatest achievement to date. It is a masterful novel, deceptive in its simplicity and ingenious in its craftsmanship. And, in linking many of the overriding themes of both *Greenvoe* and *Magnus,* his two best-known novels, it manages to transcend them both and evolve into something even greater and more profound.

In *Beside The Ocean Of Time,* eight sections take us through stages in the life of Thorfinn Ragnarson, "the laziest and most useless" boy on Norday. Thorfinn spends much of his youth in a dream world, reliving the history of his island and his people. He travels back in time to join Viking adventurers at the Byzantine court in Constantinople, falls in with a hapless knight on the way to the battle of Bannockburn and joins the broch-builders on Norday. Through Thorfinn's dreams, Mackay Brown creates a rich, complex pageant of island history and legend, that is at once both timeless and allegorical.

The very nature and significance of time itself is explored in this novel:

A wave in the Sound... crashed against the round ancient ruin on the shore, and carried away another stone that had stood for twelve centuries. That stone would trundle here and there with the tides, flung back and fore in the mill of ocean for a few decades, growing smaller and ever more spherical, until it was at last a scattering of sand among the oyster grains and the grains of crab and cormorant.

A hundred years on, and a child might be building a sandcastle on the edge of the tide, on a summer afternoon.

Out of destruction, comes rebirth. And, inevitably, the pattern of life, the cycle of existence, comes round again, unbroken and unaltered.

The cyclical nature of life and existence is a core theme in all George Mackay Brown's writing, but it is at the very heart of *Beside The Ocean Of Time*:

The chief of Norday island said to the boy Thorfinn Ragnarson (you must remember, this was long before the time of the Vikings and the Norse settlers, and Thorfinn would have had a different name then, an early Celtic name long forgotten, but it was the same boy – that much is certain)...

Throughout this extraordinary novel, through all Thorfinn's imaginings, it is "the same boy", transposed in time, but in essence and identity indistinguishable. It's a strong theme that echoes the central concern of *Magnus* – truly, nothing can happen only once. History, in all its glorious repetitions and permutations, is continually reinventing itself. Douglas Gifford once wrote of George Mackay Brown that "...his case is the sad one of a truly great writer who has chosen to live in a room with only one view from its single window." Yet it seems to me that Brown's ability to mould and craft his central concerns to fit each novel is one of his greatest strengths. He uses repetition for emphasis, not because he has run out of things to say. Nature itself is, by definition, repetitive – that's its lifeforce, its future – and, as Brown writes about nature, his style embodies it:

...they walked beside the ocean of the end and the beginning.

For Thorfinn, Norday continually reinvents itself. As he grows from boy to man, he leaves both his dreams and his island home behind, venturing into the real world. It's a world facing the harsh realities of war from which Thorfinn seeks escape once again in his imaginings. This time, however, the daydreams become something positive and concrete – Thorfinn's novel.

When he returns to Norday, nothing is as he remembers it – and yet everything is. He has to scrape a living from land and sea, a task he has never before had to perform – though his forebears have done so: "...let's hope the blood of a few generations remembers" he says to himself, as if the collective experiences of his ancestors lie dormant in the very fibre of his being.

In the end, we're left unsure as to what is real. Is it Norday, the island which still exists when all the people and farms and airstrips have gone? Is it Thorfinn and Sophie, reunited in an impossible coincidental romance? Or is it Brown, the narrator, wielding the power of his pen over the world he has created? Like the characters themselves, the reader is left trying to fit the pieces of *Beside The Ocean Of Time* into the jigsaw of life. How much of Thorfinn exists in Brown – and vice versa – is impossible to tell. But are we to believe that Brown himself feels he is nearing the end of his work?

"I won't go on much longer with this writing," he said...

"I'll dig my three acres and milk my goat," said Sophie. "I'll settle for that. We never find what we set our hearts on. We ought to be glad of that."

Only time will tell.

Frank, one of the central characters in the title story of John Herdman's *Imelda*, finds, but never attains, what he has set his heart on – but neither do any of the other characters in this dark, tragic story. Reminiscent in many ways of both Tennyson's *Maud* and Hogg's *Confessions of a Justified Sinner*, it is a story which presents multiple viewpoints, the dominant one of which belongs to Frank, a man alleged to be suffering from a mental illness. I say 'alleged', for in this story nothing is certain. We do not know whether Imelda is an innocent or a temptress, whether Uncle Affleck is hero or villain. We do not even know what Hubert's dog is called – is it 'Wing Commander' (as stated by Frank) or 'Flight Sergeant' (Uncle Affleck's assertion)?

Each narrator is the author of his or her own story – as is Thorfinn – and it is up to the reader to unravel the clues and decide what really happened to poor Hubert. *Imelda* is nightmarish in both its subject and means of narration – and yet it is completely and utterly compelling. Its theme is reality, in all its complexities – there is no one truth, no definitive answer her. There is only confusion and darkness and tragedy. There is no sense of time, either – despite searching this story for clues, I cannot discover exactly when *Imelda* takes place, perhaps because its themes of jealousy

and sibling rivalry are timeless themselves.

Fact and fiction merge in other stories in this collection, too. Characters flit from story to story – Brechin the poet reads his epic work, 'The Old Dying Sheep' in 'The Devil And Dr Tuberose' and again in 'Acquainted With Grief'. Patterns are being formed all the time to convey the never-ending, repetitive nature of experience. At the same time, Herdman seems to be inviting the reader to question what is actually real. Is it the world of 'The Day I Met The Queen Mother', a surreal story whose logic cannot be faulted? Or is it 'Herdman's Chiropractic Diary', a story that presents itself as "real", but which contains elements of the bizarre? Through all these stories, snippets of weird and banal occurrences in everyday life are juxtaposed with tragedies – a man descending into madness, another, newly released from prison, seeking security once again in violence. These moments sit uneasily with the flashes of dark humour Herdman displays – but maybe that's not so far removed from the "real" world after all.

Millions have stood on this very same ledge, in the privacy of their own homes, the unweeded gardens of their minds. Millions have stood on the edge, and tested their balance, their common sense, strength of will, they have reckoned up the cost, in mess and misery, have wondered whether below the netless drop a large tree with spread branches awaits to cushion their fall.

Like the exhausted mother in 'All The Little Loved Ones', the protagonists of *Red Tides* are people living on the edge, struggling to find their place in the world. Constantly torn between duty and escape, reality and potential, they stand on the brink, gazing at possible ways out. Most don't have the courage to step forward and risk falling – the woman in 'Over Her Head' knows that, soon, she will have to leave the quiet sanctuary of her cellar and return to her family upstairs. The singer in 'The MaMa Chorus' sinks into drunken oblivion as she grows older and her career falters. And escape, fulfilment, is within reach of the woman in 'This Is Tomorrow', but she misses her chance, defeated by her own body and its need for sleep.

Interestingly, few, if any, of the adult women in these stories have names, except when they are peripheral characters. Men do – Larry Myrtle, Malek, Charlie T'Ang – but the women are nameless, mothers, wives, lovers, universal embodiments of womanhood rather than individual people. Through these stories, they chart vast tracts of female experience – fantasising about unattainable men ('In Bed With Luis Fortuna'), undergoing surgery ('Gynae'), experiencing severe PMS ('Hormones'). These stories are concerned with human experience from a female viewpoint, and in this respect, they differ completely from Herdman's. But strip away the gender differences and a concern for the plight of the individual caught up in the patterns of life becomes apparent. For both authors, the subjective viewpoint is the only one that has validity for that individual – the reader, and the rest of the society that that individual touches, must decide for themselves what is fact, and what is fiction.

Pattern is the lifeblood of all three books, but George Mackay Brown is the master of the cyclical, timeless, enduring allegory and this, *Beside The Ocean Of Time,* is his finest work to date. *Angela Finlayson*

The School of Hard Knox

Musick Fyne: Robert Carver and the Art of Music in Sixteenth Century Scotland, D. James Ross, Mercat Press, £15.95; *The Scottish Autumn of Frederic Chopin,* Iwo & Pamela Zaluski, John Donald, £8.50; *Aly Bain: Fiddler on the Loose,* Mainstream, £14.99; *Alex: The Authorised Biography of Sir Alexander Gibson,* Conrad Wilson, Mainstream, £14.99

A nation stands in the dock facing two dire charges. The first brings a severe verdict: Scotland killed Frederick Chopin. An even more serious judgement borders on cultural genocide: Scotland killed all trace of her own renaissance music. Both conclusions are of course unsound. Chopin was doomed by tuberculosis before he came to Scotland. As to the glories of her sixteenth-century choral music, they indeed lay silent and hidden for four centuries. By no less than a chance miracle, a single choir book, the sole remnant of many once housed in abbeys and cathedrals, survived to find its way into the Advocate's Library in Edinburgh. When Chopin was in Edinburgh, few knew of its existence, and none knew its significance.

It contained the complete verifiable work of Robert Carver, a composer who ranks, as our century has slowly discovered, with the greatest of his European contemporaries. The discovery, step by step, was through the scholarship and enthusiasm of J.A. Fuller-Maitland (who in 1926 published Carver's astonishing 19-part motet *O Bone Jesu*), George Henry Farmer (who pioneered a modern performance of it in Glasgow in 1934), Kenneth Elliot (in his definitive collection *Music in Scotland 1500–1700* published in 1957), the scholarly writings of Isobel Woods, and Muriel Brown (with her complete edition of Carver's works, 1989). Carver's very existence in terms of hard dates has been until now tantalisingly elusive: it can be postulated that he lived a very long life, born probably in 1484/85, and dying in or around 1568.

In this handsome book by D. James Ross we now find Carver revealed in the full panoply of his historical and cultural context. It embraces the heyday of the Franco-Flemish school of polyphonic music of Josquin des Prez and others; the transition from High Renaissance catholicism "decoritt with crafty musick" and all its courtly splendour; the age of the reformed church and the contemporary poetry of William Dunbar, Gawain Douglas and David Lindsay; the vast span from the early reign of James IV to the flight of Mary and after.

The lavish brilliance, solemnity and awe-inspiring glories of Carver's *O Bone Jesu* and his magnificent ten-part Mass *Dum Sacrum Mysterium* rank with the highest and most refined products of all Scottish art in the medieval and renaissance periods. Mr Ross not only provides a full account of Carver's art and a resumé of all we know of him and his time, but devotes a goodly part of his book to tracing parallel Scottish musicians and composers, and developments in choral, instrumental and secular music through to the departure of James VI to England. If it here becomes a tragic survey of the "apogee, decline and death of a culture" as Jamie Reid Baxter's foreword has it, then the book is also a tale of "life and light, an illumination of the past that creates a source of inspiration for the present and the future."

We must see past Knox. We can now *hear* beyond him to that age of luminosity that has lain long in dark eclipse. That clarity and breadth of Ross's test is enhanced by twenty-five monochrome and four colour plates and over fifty musical examples. A work of beauty and scholarship, it will long be of seminal importance to readers of both musical and general Scottish history.

Among Chopin's lesser piano works are three Ecossaises. They were not however directly inspired by Scotland, being composed in Paris years before his three-month Scottish visit of 1848. During that autumn he played Scots tunes to entertain his fashionable and kindly hosts at a succession of country houses, and wrote of hearing some "pretty Scotch airs" sung and played by villagers near Edinburgh. But nothing he heard or strummed moved him to compose, and during the whole of his Scottish stay he created nothing of significance. This fact, together with his debilitating illness, the deteriorating weather, and an increasing irritation with his well-intentioned but demanding hosts, depressed him considerably. Iwo and Pamela Zaluski re-tell the familiar sad tale and describe the localities with engaging attention to detail. A slim volume, it adds little to musicology, but may afford the wry reflection that Scottish musical history of that time is highlighted by such foreign visitations – Mendelssohn, Paganini and Liszt had preceded Chopin – just because nothing was stirring on the native soil.

In the twentieth century Scotland's music has again reached out to the whole world. In the case of Aly Bain, internationality began with a step *to* the Scottish mainland – for the extraordinary fiddle player who dazzled Edinburgh in 1969 and was touring abroad for the next year, is of course a Shetlander. As Alastair Clark notes in his lively and colourfully-illustrated biography, "For Aly, and for many Shetlanders, mainland Scotland was almost foreign territory... with strange-sounding names and even stranger ways of living." And with all the triumphs shared with the Boys of the Lough, the taking by storm of Carnegie Hall and other Olympiads in the far east and further west, it is to Shetland, musically and spiritually, that this star who has embraced folk, country, rock and jazz, consistently and resoundingly returns.

Forty years ago, no one could have foreseen the achievements for Scottish music and opera that were opened up by one man, Sir Alexander Gibson, whose recent death has robbed us all too soon of a much-loved, shy, quiet, yet resolutely influential figure. Conrad Wilson's book took his story to the end of 1992 and now leaves the feeling that much more could be said about this reticent yet most resourceful of conductors. Inevitably it will be: the internal climate of politics and decision-making that led to Alex's departure from Scottish Opera (which he co-founded) is not an area which he himself would have lost dignity to carp about in public, and Wilson deals with the episode tactfully. The (Royal) SNO – a good orchestra that its first native-born conductor raised to international greatness – also brought him subsequent heartbreak. Yet that was not the end of the story. A robustness that had seen him recruit a new bold Edinburgh Festival Chorus, popularise concerts through proms in Glasgow and Edinburgh, above all champion new music both in the opera house and through the Musica Viva and Musica Nova series of concerts, served to widen his horizons to the last. Personally I owe to him my first and unforgettable hearings of great cycles of Sibelius, Henze, Wagner and a host of 'moderns'. A younger generation is, perhaps unknowingly, much in debt to him. This book is more than just a catalogue of achievement: its subject shines through every page as a sensitive and unselfish human being who left Scotland a better place than he found it and, thanks to him, immeasurably richer in musical resources.   *Derek Watson*

East by North-East

New York Times, Sudeep Sen, The Many Press, £6.95; *Shoah*, Harry Smart, Faber, £9.95; *Nil Nil*, Don Paterson, Faber, £5.99

New York may have inspired great verse from American poets as different as Hart Crane, Allen Ginsberg and Bob Dylan but it often stuns visiting writers into cliche. Even Norman MacCaig was reduced to writing about "Jumbo-sized dentists's drills" and "glittering canyons" in response to his visit to Manhattan, described in his 1968 collection *Rings on a*

Tree. The Indian writer Sudeep Sen, until recently the Poet in Residence at the Scottish Poetry Library, generally avoids such traps in *New York Times*, a sequence of poems about his time spent in Manhattan as a graduate student at Columbia University. Only once, in 'Night in Times Square', does he fall back on familiar sentiments:

> in the glass and steel canyon
> of downtown, in the city of dreams.

Elsewhere Sen seems to have an original take on New York. Describing Greenwich Village, where Manhattan's grid system of streets and avenues breaks down into confusion, he notes "Nowhere else would you be able to find, for example, West 4th Street bisecting West 12th Street." That breaking down of systems makes Greenwich Village like "old parts of other cities where neighbourhoods and street patterns naturally grew with time and changed with history, and history this area certainly has." His pleasure in exploring the ancient side of New York marks him out from most visitors who are bewildered by what they see as its brash novelty. But Sen is not just a visitor from an older culture, enjoying that part of New York which in its old-world jumble, seems most familiar to him, he is a visiting writer, and is fascinated by the other writers who have temporarily made New York their home. 'Greenwich Village', a prose memoir in this poetic sequence, gives the reader the street addresses of Edith Wharton, Edna St Vincent Millay and Dylan Thomas. That eclectic mix of authorial talent indicated Sen's other dominant sense of New York: that it is a radical mix of other cultures. Though that point has been made before, Sen's title poem makes it again charmingly, almost whimsically as the poet begins the day by fleeing "past the red and white awning of the Jewish deli,/ walk out with a bagel or croissant or spilled coffee,/ disappearing underground in a flurry".

Appropriately, his model for the visitor's response to the variety of cultures in New York is one of consumption: where will the food I eat today come from? This collection itself displays a fine sense of cultural variety. The aphoristic quotations from other writers which situate Sen's poems are a mixture of comments from American insiders, Saul Bellow, Alan Ross and Donald Hall, and outsiders P.G. Wodehouse, H.G. Wells and Agha Shahid Ali, in varying states of bemusement or awe at beholding New York. Sen manages to situate himself skilfully between insider- and outsider-dom, responding to his adopted city with a firm blend of sympathy and detachment. That seems to ally him with another Indian writing in English, Vikram Seth, whose *Golden Gate* celebrated San Francisco in octosyllabic rhyming verse. But whereas Seth immersed himself in San Francisco and showed us its foibles from the inside, Sen retains the virtues of a sensitive and perceptive visitor to New York.

A less successful travelogue forms part of *Shoah*, Harry Smart's second collection of verse which follows the successful *Pierrot*. The title sequence is taken from the Hebrew word for destruction, and Smart's book is constructed out of three sequences. The first is a collection of personal poems set in Germany of the present day, the second a small set of translations from the German poet Rainer Malkowski, and the third, 'Shoah' itself, is set on a boat in an empty world, as a reconstruction of the story of Genesis. What holds the three sections loosely together is the experience of Jews in Germany during the 1930s and 1940s.

The first sequence of poems make up a succession of rather fleeting and unsatisfying portraits of present-day Germany. The memories his visits provoke are described in 'Frohmut':

> It's August 1955, and my first trip abroad.
> It's a trip I still know nothing about
> apart from what my mother's told me.
> What I remember's constructed.

Though this poem opens up an interesting space for the poet to explore in the construction of memory, little is made of it. The poems in this opening sequence tend to be unfocused and so personal as to have little resonance.

Smart's great virtue as a poet is his characteristic tone, which at its best can be limpid and timeless. This gift is applied to successful effect in the 'Shoah' sequence, especially in individual poems like 'It was late', and 'We sat and counted'. What seems less successful and less wise, is to create, as an archetypal negative to the dove which plays such a significant part in the Genesis story, a Crow figure. Smart's Crow is unfortunately unable to differentiate itself from that of his Faber stable-mate Ted Hughes, and Hughes' distinctive style seems to take over those poems in which the Crow appears. Smart's Crow

> ... clacks his beak, swoops in for a fat insect,
> Gollops it down.
> Take more than a flood to get rid of old Crow.

is rather too close for comfort to Hughes' Crow,

> Screaming for Blood
> Grubs, crusts
> Anything

This curious influence seems to be typical of the collection as a whole, which never settles in a distinctive and confident voice. Though in his stride Smart has a powerful and recognisable style, in *Shoah* he never seems to reach it.

Don Paterson's *Nil Nil* must be one of the most confident and successful first collections of poetry published in the last twenty years. From the first poem, 'The Ferryman's Arms', Paterson shows a winning combination of strong, muscular verse-forms and a long imaginative reach. In 'Exeunt', a sequence of deaths are described in metaphors drawn out from the lives of the dying. 'Drop Serene' has the man who makes transparent moulds, which contain arrangements of wasps and flowers, being engulfed by

> the blank wall of water that always kept pace,
> glittering an inch, half an inch from his back.
> He was out in the garden, digging the borders
> when it caught him, in a naturalistic pose.

And the poem 'Electric Brae' from the same sequence makes a daring metaphorical connection between the life support apparatus which sustains the existence of the father in the hospital bed, and "the terrible jug band/ now reduced to a wheezy concertina." That poem ends with the movement of a car on the electric brae, surging uphill, and the moment of release from life.

Paterson's persona in these poems is strongly and unsentimentally masculine. He describes sex, drinking, pishing, and explores the relationship with his father. The poem 'An Elliptical Stylus' describes the petty humiliation of his father by a gramophone salesman who points out that to make their turntable sound better they'll have to do more than just buy a new stylus:

> Still smirking, he sent us from the shop
> with a box of needles, thick as carpet-tacks,
> the only sort they made to fit our model.

That poem toys with the poem which the writer would have written if his upbringing had been different and then turns at the end not only on the salesman, but on the assumptions of the reader:

> I'd swing for him, and every other cunt
> happy to let my father know his station,
> which probably includes yourself, to be blunt.

That moment steps into the territory delineated by Tony Harrison in his poems about his father, but then Paterson decisively claims it for himself. If the title of this poem also suggests that the poet is an elliptical sty*list* it is a suitable choice, for Paterson's poems often approach their true subjects from unusual angles. With that in mind it seems interesting that the one failure in this book is the poem 'Graffito', which is playful and sexually explicit, but rather pointless.

Paterson's background as a musician can be seen not only in an ease with metaphors to do with musical instruments, but in an absolute confidence about using the long verse line, varying the stresses within in a way which makes his verse both sinuous and certain. That, combined with a fine thematic range of poems make this work seem less like a first book, and more like the work of an established major writer.

Though Paterson titles his book after a no-score draw he's certain to enjoy a quick rise to the top of the Premier Division.

David Stenhouse

Theatre Roundup

Everybody was saying that Mayfest wasn't the same this year, that something of that proletarian spirit had gone from it, that easy-oasy character. The Fest, as masterminded by Paul Bassett had lost contact with its roots. Certainly I noticed that there was a certain buzz lacking, that excitement, a feeling of a festival grounded in something other than the elitist arts. But my Mayfest was really located at the Tron, as it happens, which had an extremely good festival, and I had no opportunity to trawl the peripheral events, and so I can only relate others' observations.

At the Tron there were some unforgettable things, especially Theatre Du Kronope's *Notre Dame de Paris,* Victor Hugo as you've never seen him done. The verbal dexterity of the actors is only outdone by their physical agility, as they re-enact the tragic story on an inspired set, a raised, rounded platform suggesting the roofs of the Cathedral, punctuated with unlikely portals through which the actors emerge by various interesting means. There was only one thing lacking: the pathos of the story, but otherwise it was a fascinating visual, dramatic spectacle and a positive triumph of teamwork, physical theatre at its best.

If Scotland lacks a continuous dramatic tradition there is only one thing it can and should do: look westward, and yes, you can see Ireland from these shores. *The Mai* is a play by that neglected Irish playwright Marina Carr, a play which both evokes the human problems of modern Ireland but set firmly in the loam of Irish tradition and legend. There are some unforgettable characters in it, notably Grandma Fraochlain, the drink-swilling, eccentric incorrigible old woman who at the age of 90 something is still trying out new drugs – magnificently played by Joan O'Hara, but not detracting from an elegant performance by Olwen Fouere as The Mai, a woman in her early 40s whose estranged, opportunistic husband suddenly decides to rejoin her. There was a dignity, a poise, an assurance about the whole production which Scottish theatre could learn much from.

Liz Lochhead was there too, with her own company's version of *Tartuffe,* a rollicking, raunchy affair which was impossible not to enjoy, working in the best tradition of uninhibited Scottish farce. Tartuffe himself was played with splendidly self-righteous sleaziness by Sandy Welch in a performance in which much more than his grey cardigan will resonate. It was *The Broons* or *Oor Wullie* brought to the footlights, minus, of course, the pail, but such a delightfully irreverent piece.

Born Guilty was the new production from 7:84, given minimal houseroom at the Citz. The play, culled from books by Peter Sichrovsky, attempted to deal with the legacy of World War Two for the German people, here I come, guilty or not, a montage performance from actors dressed largely in grey. The first act had its *longueurs*, with too much of the 'stand up and pronounce it from here to the audience' method, but the second half focused powerfully on the various issues and responses, giving an integrity to the production which otherwise lacked the leavening of humour, being over-strait laced and serious in a tunnel-visioned kind of way.

7:84 could have taken a leaf or two from Wiseguise production of *Asylum Asylum* by Irish playwright Donal O'Kelly, not strictly speaking part of Mayfest, but around at the same time. Concerning the fate of an illegal immigrant from Uganda, Joseph, the play never forgot its human side

On the downside there was *The Collection,* a new and eagerly awaited play by Mike Cullen about debt collection, which never succeeded in touching the human chord at all. It resounded with patter of the worst sort, guaranteed to keep the Glasgow audience at the Tron tittering, but never touching the heart of the subject. The script was incredibly indulgent and the Traverse production definitely on automatic pilot with a smart but shallow presentation which never touched, never mind penetrated the surface. There is a very real and horrible play to be written about this subject, but this wasn't it: the playwright was too busy entertaining the audience with one-liners, rather than revealing the torture and anguish caused by such situations.

Brilliant Traces by Cindy Lou Johnson both tried to and succeeded in penetrating surfaces, about a bride who took sudden flight in full wedding attire and drove just a couple of thousand miles to Alaska, to arrive in mid-white-out at a poor reclusive oil-man's door. A dramatic beginning, shall we say, and the danger of the situation was never allowed to escape the audience's attention in this Diva production, a new woman's company directed ably by Caroline Hall. The Scottish actor Fiona Bell has been the recipient of much praise recently, but I must say that her performance in this was a very workaday one, monodimensional and uninspired in spite of the throwing of herself about the stage at certain points. Never mind that: The level of imagination engaged by the production was of the highest order.

I wish I could say the same for Wildcat's *Bedfellows*, which was a travesty of a farce if ever I saw one. It played to the worst Scottish instincts, the kailyard pseudo-Highland sensibilities of *Brigadoon*, and included unforgivably lifeless caricatures of the likes of the late Sir Nicholas Fairbairn, who must fair be birlin in his grave in irritation. The plot was, to say the least, thin, over the ownership of a Perthshire hotel and the circumstantial fate of those who might bide for a night or two. It was a farce of a farce, addressing issues in Scotland which have been long put to rest, and with the usual Wildcat socialist propaganda which needs a thorough shake-up.

One of the best things I've seen in a long time was Communicado's touring production of *Tall Tales for Small People*, stagings of three stories by traveller-storyteller Duncan Williamson. The stories themselves are full of eventful life and magic: in 'The Hunchback and the Swan' a hunchback is pining for love of a swan, and is eventually transmogrified into a swan so as to be able to be with her forever. The language used was very much the language of the original stories, a vibrant, energetic Scots, entirely faithful to the originals, delivered with great competence by the cast. What was so remarkable about the production was the teamwork of the actors who gave themselves with relish to the vitality of the stories. Their reward was an audience entirely spellbound by the stories: I've never seen an audience of children paying such close attention. Most of all, Gerry Mulgrew was giving them material which in no way patronised them: it was life in the raw. In one of the stories a childbirth takes place on stage,

and no attempt was made to sanitise the process or magic it away.

David Harrower's new play at the Traverse, *Knives in Hens* was set in 16th century Scotland and attempted to portray real characters surviving in that very basic economy. A three-hander, a simple story about a ploughman Pony William and his wife, and their fretful relationship with Gilbert the Miller, which develops later into a love-triangle. It may be loosely based on a folk-tale: certainly there are tales which cover the territory, but what was most interesting about it was the use of language. Harrower is attempting a rural equivalent of something like Iain Heggie's staccato urban dialogue. The use of words is plain, unadorned, cast not in Scots (why?) but in a Scottish voice. Apparently the author is under some misapprehension that in 16th century Scotland words were few, and in the process of being invented to cope with new phenomena, which rather underestimates the intellectual subtlety of Scots at that period. One of the most powerful aspects of *Knives in Hens* was its strong location in and relation of the characters in the elements: land, sea, sky, nature and that relationship comes over as uncompromising and difficult.

Perhaps the most moving production I've seen lately is *Shoot the Crow* by Jolt Theatre Company, staged in Perth's studio theatre. The actors, apart from two, were severely disabled, but the play made no attempt to mask or understate their condition, instead used it to orchestrate the play. In a highly disciplined way the actors created complex visual patterns on the stage, and in the course of the play each one told his or her own story. In the methods employed, the play was genuinely avant-garde, but the audience were completely drawn in despite the strangeness of it, the fact that not all was immediately comprehensible: you didn't have to understand – it was a privilege to observe. I almost choked when one of the actors announced: "I want flair, I want imagination, fragrance, peace, justice. I want to live." This simple, direct statement carried utter integrity, as did the rest of the production. Clearly the disabled actors had collaborated fully in the creation of the peace, which I fervently hope will be seen again somewhere.

Joy Hendry

Pamphleteer

Welcome is tangible hot air
like a cuff in the face
(Thirty-three years is a long time)

So begins a series of poems exploring John Lyons' return to his native Trinidad in *Behind the Carnival* (£6.95, Smith/Doorstop Books, The Studio, Byram Arcade, Westgate, Huddersfield, HD1 1ND). These poems combine an insider's view of the Caribbean with the more distanced perspective of exile, and the result is a collection packed with rich and sparkling images. Although some of Lyons' observations lack originality, his picture of the Trinidadian life which he has left behind is compelling. The simultaneous energy and languor of the Caribbean infuses his poetry. In 'Return', for example, he describes

... the swell of energy
the exuberance of words, colourful
as Assynan's fabric stores on Charlotte Street,
the urge to spree still burning
unruly as flambeaux in the wind;
the calypso heartbeat
in the way the body moves.

The different worlds of Britain and Trinidad collide in one of the funniest poems in the collection, 'Mother's Milk'. Refuting his lover's complaint that he doesn't understand women, the poet describes an incident from his childhood when a neighbouring woman squirted breast milk into his eye to soothe a pain. The lover's response to this revelation? "'WELL,' she says, flouncing out of bed / 'that explains A LOT!'".

Also from Smith/Doorstop, *Trying On Their Souls For Size* by Joan Jobe Smith, and *14 Ways Of Listening To The Archers* by Cliff Yates (both £2.95). Most of the poems in Smith's collection revolve around memories of her mother and father. 'On her way to heaven', for example, is a moving portrait of the poet's dying mother, while the following poem, 'Subsequence', looks at the way the three years spent looking after her sick mother is viewed suspiciously by prospective employers. The personal, emotional tone of these poems becomes somewhat wearing by the end, and left me longing for something sharper to cut through the nostalgia. In contrast is the rather surreal collection from Cliff Yates. This includes poems about lawnmowers catching fire, stargazing on a sunlounger in the frost, and a meeting with prospective in-laws which goes horribly wrong when the protagonist accidentally kicks their budgie into the fire. Quite entertaining.

Fish Oil (£3, City of Aberdeen Arts and Recreation Division, Central Library, Rosemount Viaduct, Aberdeen, AB9 1GU) is the result of Aberdeen Writer in Residence Todd McEwen's attempt to discover the literary talents of young people in the city. The three writers whose work appears here – Giles de Burgh, Peter Forbes and Michelle Moore – present us with their views of the city in verse and prose, and, as McEwen warns, it "isn't always a pleasant journey around town". The contributions range from de Burgh's bald statement of a poem "Winter, autumn, spring/ summer is non-existent/ in cold Aberdeen" to Forbes' long and unsubtle diatribe against single mothers. Although there are flashes of wit, all three exhibit not the "fierce determination to see" that McEwen promises, but a retreat into kneejerk criticism. A brave attempt on the part of the city of Aberdeen to publish the critical opinions of young people, which fails to live up to its potential.

The cynicism of David Crystal's poetry in *The Beetle House* (£2.50, Clocktower Press, 27 Alfred Street, Stromness, Orkney, KW16 3DF), in contrast, is carefully directed and well executed. The title poem chillingly describes the life of Mr Beetle, a man who can be seen "exchanging shoes with some dosser / at Leicester Square / then stealing his bag of chips". His hobby is "impersonating the relatives/ of the deceased" on cancer wards, and he spends his evenings playing computer chess. These poems are about the chasm between expectation and reality in today's society:

Her essay 'Poverty and Crime
in the 1930s'
clinched a 2:1, with Honours.
Rummaging through
plastic shoes
with the dregs of a giro
everything
started to make
perfect
sense.

The Minister's Cat (Scottish Cultural Press,

£4.95), written by Douglas Kynoch and illustrated by Norman Glen, describes itself as "An A–Z of cats in verse". Based on the parlour game 'The Minister's Cat', there are 26 poems, the first about an Ambitious cat, the second about a Benevolent cat, the third about a Canny cat, and so on. A little twee, but I liked the front cover pastiche of Raeburn's painting, involving a very stately-looking cat skating on Duddingston loch...

Hughie Healy's first book of poetry, *Who needs orgasms!* (£3.95, Neruda Press, 51 Allison Street, Glasgow, G42 8JN), is full of gritty poems about Glaswegian life. This collection could certainly benefit from some serious editing, as Healy's tendency to ramble around a subject often reduces the impact of his writing. Despite this, his ironical twists at the end of many of these poems are often spot-on, and his playful use of language highlights his sense of anger and social injustice effectively. His ability to realise and laugh at his own prejudices and shortcomings leads to some of the more entertaining poems in the book, as in the following extract from 'Ummee':

> She brought her culture and mystique
> To my city street
> This Asian mother and child
> ...Her lips moved
> In prayer perhaps
> To a different god than mine
> The little one spoke words
> I failed to comprehend
> She answered
> In the universal language of mothers
> *I'm oot withoot any money*
> *So shut your face*
> *You're getting nae crisps!*

Sauce (£5.95, Bloodaxe Books) is the latest collection from the Poetry Virgins, a group of female performance writers and actors. Most of the poems in this collection are written by Julia Darling and Ellen Phethean. I particularly liked Phethean's "Poetry Is Fashion":

> Poems will be short this year.
> The adaptable haiku
> can be a sparkling seventeen syllables
> of silver lamé or a sombre three lines
> of grey and charcoal
> ...New poetry, with a natural look,
> aggressively-now verse
> and careful cut of rhythms,
> has sent a frisson
> through the High Street names.

Julia Darling's eye for the surreal detail is apparent in a trilogy of poems entitled 'Men on Trains', in which she describes a man in a suit "so pressed it's dead" who dabs perfume on his wrists every half hour, and another who makes odd calls on his mobile phone pretending to be in hospital. Her poem about "white male southern students", 'Be Kind', also made me laugh, as she implores the reader not to shudder at their purchases of "Pot Noodles, Fray Bentos, Vesta and peas", because

> Perhaps they are homesick, worrying about
> their parents' divorces, and yesterday's essay.
> Or have agonising lovebites on tender shoulders.
> Or are wishing they had gone to Exeter, or Bath.

Finally, also new from Bloodaxe, is Joolz's *The Pride of Lions* (£6.95). In a break from her usual performance poetry, Joolz turns in this book to writing 'short shorts', pointed and compelling portraits of contemporary life. Many of the stories are about people who are trapped within the confines of their lives, some longing for the chance to escape, others content to make the best of themselves, others unable to realise that they are trapped at all. In 'The Lilac' we see Susie trying to defend her own mundane life against the glamour of her sister's travels and adventures. The smallness of lives is a recurring theme in this collection, and Joolz portrays such lives with compassion and understanding. The description of Tracy, in a story of the same name, is an affectionate picture of a fifteen-year-old girl, pregnant and holding forth to her friends on the bus about her forthcoming wedding. The storyteller pictures her "hapless bridegroom":

> What gormless Darren, Steve or Gaz strayed into Tracy's hands one hot night at the Youthie and became a daddy at 16. Too witless to make the connection, he passed from his mother to his wife without visible effort.

These stories are littered with arresting descriptions, from the neighbour who "has a husband rather in the way some people are haunted" to the young mother who tortures her son in a cafe: "It's the only way she ever feels any control in her life, through the certainty of his childish terror and all the glib, distancing jargon of the chattering classes can't comprehend the dumb, fucking cruelty of it".
A treat.   *Julie McCulloch*

Catalogue

It won't take you long to read Fred D'Aguiar's *The Longest Memory* (Chatto, £9.99) and you'll be glad you did. Woven from editorials in 1810 editions of *The Virginian*, the novel dramatises the tragedy of slavery in intensely personal terms – first-person narratives from each of the several protagonists. Short, to the point, horrifying and immensely resonant, it lends a different perspective to *A Dance Called America* (Mainstream, £14.99), James Hunter's story of Gaelic Scotland's impact on the development of North America. This is a compelling narrative, long on thoroughly-researched fact and short on sentimentality. Although there is a moral basis to Hunter's critique, its strength lies in an awareness of conflicting forces and complex motivations which change over the centuries, as different strands of Gaelic society are assimilated into New World culture in different ways.

A similar clear-eyed unsentimentality and depth of research, allied to considerable story-telling skill, makes Alison Prince's biography of Kenneth Grahame, *An Innocent in the Wild Wood* (Allison & Busby, £17.99) stand out from the usual tedious fare the genre offers – the PC Plod Report style satirised in one contribution to *Lord Gnome's Literary Companion* (ed Francis Wheen, Verso, £16.95), culled from *Private Eye*'s Literary Review section, kennel of the pompous, the jealous, the back-biting, the anti-intellectual, and often very funny, literary bitch.

For the writer who aspires, one day, to be so successful as to merit the *Eye*'s attention, Thomas & Lochar publish the *Writer's News Library of Writing*: a series of guidebooks on a variety of topics, including *Successful Article Writing* by Gillian Thornton, *Writing Proposals & Synopses that Sell* by André Jute, *How to Write for Children* by Marion Hough, and *Writing Poetry* by Doris Corti. Ranging in price from £8.95 to £11.95, they offer plenty of useful practical advice. Don't expect to find any magical shortcuts, however.

Heinemann's Asian Writers Series "intends to introduce English language readers to some of the interesting fiction written in languages that most will neither know nor study". Alas, the six titles launching the series share an old-fashioned narrative that suggests the average reader's fancy might remain untickled. On the other hand, from Tagore's *Quartet*, first published in 1916, to Susham Bedi's *The Fire Sacrifice*, the most recent title, published in 1989 and set in New York, the selection ranges interestingly over time and place – Shaukat Osman's *Janani* in pre-partition Bengal; Ashokamitran's *Water* in Madras, 1969. Altaf Fatima's *The One Who Did Not Ask* among the Muslim upper classes; T Sivasankra Pillai's *Scavenger's Son* among the harijan caste.

That old-fashionedness, or is it Social Realism? characterises George Friel's novel *The Bank of Time*, originally published in 1959, now reissued by Polygon (£8.95). The tale of three youngsters maturing in tenement Glasgow, its narrative style seems curiously reminiscent of the patronising genre in children's fiction. Relentlessly determined to impress the reader with how right-on hip streetwise etc etc he is *in spite of adverse circumstances*, Tom Morton's *Red Guitars in Heaven* (Mainstream, £7.99) comes over as thinly disguised autobiography, or rather day-dream journal. "Cheerfully nasty", as the publicity has it.

The Shugathon chugs on: two more volumes in the MacDiarmid 2000 collection from Carcanet in *Lucky Poet* and the second volume of the *Complete Poems*. More of a collector's item than the first volume, which contains the majority of the great works, Volume 2 nevertheless includes *In Memoriam James Joyce*, the third Hymn to Lenin, *The Kind of Poetry I Want* and *Dìreadh*. *Lucky Poet* is apparently a quarter of the length it was originally intended to be. Phew. Scotsoun's recording of *Sangschaw* and *Penny Wheep* with Tom Fleming and Iain Cuthbertson among the readers is excellent value at £6.35 (from 13 Ashton Place, Glasgow G12 8SP). More recently they have produced a double kistie of Alastair Mackie (£11) and, for the first time, a tape of translations between Scots and Gaelic, *Twa Leids/Dà Chànan* (£13.50) with a full text. Let's slip in a couple more excellent kisties: *Parallel*, selected poems of Sudeep Sen from the Scottish Poetry Library, where Sen was poet in residence during the winter of '92–'93, and *Competent at Peever* by Liz Lochhead, from Book Trust Scotland (£7.50). From the same source, four

Scottish poetry posters beautifully marrying image and verse – 'Pushing Forty' (Alison Fell) with *Beeches in Glen Lyon* (Iain Cheyne); 'The Black Boat' (Sorley MacLean) with *Landscape at Kyleakin* (Anne Redpath); 'The Bonnie Broukit Bairn' (Hugh MacDiarmid) with *The Harvest Moon* (Charles Rennie Mackintosh); and 'Scotland' (Alastair Reid) with *Crofts, Bonar Bridge* (William Gillies).

There's no doubt that Jack Vettriano's paintings make forceful impressions. His deceptive realist style, with starkly-lit figures foregrounded by plain backdrops, recalls the profoundly lonely paintings of Edward Hopper. Not everyone can stomach the power-relationships between clothed male and unclothed female that recur in his work; perhaps such people lack a sense of humour. It's all on display in *Fallen Angels*, a collection of Vettriano pictures set alongside poetry and prose from the likes of Burns and Stevenson on the one hand, and specially-written contributions from the likes of Jack Gerson, Joy Hendry, Alan Taylor, Sue Glover on the other, edited by W. Gordon Smith and sold by Pavilion for a very reasonable £16.99. From Thomas & Lochar, at the more usual art-book price of £39, comes *Painters of Scotland: a celebration of Scottish Landscape* by Vivienne Couldrey, which essays a history of landscape painting in Scotland, mingling judicious use of photographs with a large number of delicious reproductions.

It's interesting to note, leafing through *Scottish Ballads* (ed Emily Lyle, Canongate Classics, £4.99), how many of them would be familiar to followers of the English folk-rock scene back in the 1970s – Tam Lin, The Fause Knight, Wee Messgrove etc etc – ballads don't respect borders. A bonus in *Gàir nan Clàrsach* (Birlinn, £10.99) is that Colm Ó Baoill's selection of seventeenth century Gaelic poetry (with parallel translations by Meg Bateman) is complemented in many cases by melody.

A Stuggy Pren is a new collection of poetry, prose and bits and pieces by Ivor Cutler, with photographs by Katrina Lithgow (Arc Publications, £7.95). Some vintage Cutler: "For the eighty metre race, I laid down a track starting seventy metres from the edge of the cliff, and placed a man to shout 'Ten metres to go!' at the edge..." *Young Poets of Germany* (ed Uwe-Michael Gutzschhahn & translated by Raymond Hargreaves, Forest Books, £10.95) captures something of the mood among young intellectuals around the time of reunification. Lotte Kramer's *The Desecration of Trees* (Hippopotomus Press, £7.95) is her third collection: delicately-made and assured, and a well-designed book into the bargain. Like Kramer, Raymond Tong has graced the pages of *Chapman* in his time: after a life spent overseas in education and British Council work, his *Selected Poems* (Robert Hale, £10.95) covers a lot of territory. Also, Eric Ratcliffe, editor of *Ore*, has *Fire in the Bush*, his collected poems over 40 years, available from 7 The Towers, Southgate, Stevenage SG1 1HE (Cheques for £5 payable to James Hogg)

Mary McCabe's novel *Everwinding Times* (Argyll Publishing, £6.99) is a little ponderous in narrative style, but given the central character, Ailie Lorimer, is (apparently) suffering from amnesia, and the novel consequently plays cleverly with time, pushing an allegory of marginalisation, who's in a hurry? Speaking of marginalisation, ENGENDER's Gender Audit 1994 (c/o Scottish Women's Aid, 12 Torphichen Street, Edinburgh EH3 8JQ) contains lots of statistics on the position of women in contemporary Scottish society. Hopefully future reports will present statistics in graphic form: rows of numbers are difficult to digest.

Two Old Women is a traditional story of betrayal and tragedy turning to courage and strength from the Athabaska tribe of Alaska, committed to print here with elegant beauty by Velma Wallis (Women's Press, £5.99). Also from the Women's Press, the unique craft and integrity of Alice Walker in *The Complete Stories*. (£15.99).

If you aren't put off by having to look up the title in a dictionary, or by seeing the name of the mountebank Lacan on the back cover, *The Metastases of Enjoyment* (Verso, £12.95) is an amusing collection of essays 'on Woman and Causality' by Slavoj Zizek, which toss you around like some sorry little boat on a turbulent ocean of cultural references from Derrida to David Lynch. It's hard to keep a straight face reading earnest analyses of minutiae in the latter's film of *Dune* – *Très* Derrida – but it's stimulating, too.

Notes on Contributors

Shanta Acharya: born in India, educated at Oxford and Harvard, now an investment manager in London. Her first collection of poetry, *Not This, Not That*, was recently published by Rupa in India.

Ron Butlin has published seven books. *Histories of Desire*, a new collection of poetry, will be out in October 1995. He lives in Edinburgh with his wife and their dog.

Elspeth Davie: b Ayrshire 1919; attended Edinburgh College of Art; one of Scotland's most distinguished post-war writers.

Alistair Findlay is a social work manager in Livingston, "a native of West Lothian, a former Hibs signing, a former communist, writing a family-community history of Shale, looking forwards, over my shoulder."

Angela Finlayson, an occasional Chapman volunteer, works for DC Thompson and lives in Fife.

Paula Fitzpatrick: b Glasgow 1951, is a graduate of Glasgow School of Art, now a civil servant.

Penny Glenday: freelance writer and book reviewer – amongst other things.

Alasdair Gray's contribution will appear in a book called *Agnes Belfrage and Five Other Stories* from Bloomsbury in 1996. His most recent novel, *A History Maker*, is published by Canongate.

Andrew Hamilton: b Greenock, 1921. Reared in Clydebank, trained, and spent life, in production engineering. Now striving to produce literary works.

Ann Lingard lived in Glasgow but is now exiled in Oxford. She is a freelance broadcaster, has had several short stories published, and has just finished her second novel.

Manfred Malzahn, b 1955 in West Germany, to a fairly international family, including a Scottish branch; currently professor of English and German in Chia-yi, Taiwan.

John McInnes: born and bred in Glasgow. "Brought out my 'slim volume' of poetry which I sold on the Playfair Steps in Edinburgh Festival time." Looks forward to writing more poetry in the future.

Dougie McKenzie lives & teaches in Leith, and writes short stories for fun. Recently 'Mr and Mrs' appeared in *A Tongue in yer heid*.

Vladimir Orlov: student at the Foreign Languages department of Volgograd Pedagogical University. His *Letters From Russia* is available at $7.95 from JVC Books, Rt 2, Box 440c, Arcadia, FL33821, USA

William Oxley, poet and philosopher, has also worked as an accountant, gardener and actor. Recent collections include *In the Drift of Words* (Rockingham) and *Cardboard Troy* (Stride).

Tom Pow lives and works in Dumfries. He was Scottish–Canadian Exchange Fellow in 1992/93.

John Saul has had some forty stories published in the UK, France, Italy and Germany; and a novel, *Heron and Quin*; with more coming this year.

David Stenhouse is one of BBC Radio Scotland's *Usual Suspects*.

Derek Watson: b Edinburgh 1948. Lives in Peeblesshire and is a freelance author, composer, pianist, lecturer and broadcaster.

Christopher Whyte lectures in Scottish literature at Glasgow University. He is editing *Gendering the Nation*, a collection of essays on gender and sexualities in modern Scottish literature, due from EUP later this year.